NOBEL LECTURES IN LITERATURE

1968–1980

NOBEL LECTURES

INCLUDING PRESENTATION SPEECHES
AND LAUREATES' BIOGRAPHIES

PHYSICS

CHEMISTRY

PHYSIOLOGY OR MEDICINE

LITERATURE

PEACE

ECONOMIC SCIENCES

NOBEL LECTURES

INCLUDING PRESENTATION SPEECHES AND LAUREATES' BIOGRAPHIES

LITERATURE

1968–1980

EDITOR-IN-CHARGE

TORE FRÄNGSMYR
Uppsala University, Sweden

EDITOR

STURE ALLÉN
Swedish Academy, Stockholm

World Scientific
Singapore • New Jersey • London • Hong Kong

Published for the Nobel Foundation in 1993 by

World Scientific Publishing Co. Pte. Ltd.
P O Box 128, Farrer Road, Singapore 9128
USA office: Suite 1B, 1060 Main Street, River Edge, NJ 07661
UK office: 73 Lynton Mead, Totteridge, London N20 8DH

NOBEL LECTURES IN LITERATURE (1968–1980)

ISBN 981-02-1174-0
ISBN 981-02-1175-9 (pbk)

Printed in Singapore.

FOREWORD

Since 1901 the Nobel Foundation has published annually "Les Prix Nobel" with reports from the Nobel Award Ceremonies in Stockholm and Oslo as well as the biographies and Nobel lectures of the laureates. In order to make the lectures available to people with special interests in the different prize fields the Foundation gave Elsevier Publishing Company the right to publish in English the lectures for 1901–1970, which were published in 1964–1972 through the following volumes:

Physics 1901–1970	4 vols.
Chemistry 1901–1970	4 vols.
Physiology or Medicine 1901–1970	4 vols.
Literature 1901–1967	1 vol.
Peace 1901–1970	3 vols.

Elsevier decided later not to continue the Nobel project. It is therefore with great satisfaction that the Nobel Foundation has given World Scientific Publishing Company the right to bring the series up to date beginning with the Prize lectures in Economics in 2 volumes 1969–1990. Thereafter the lectures in all the other prize fields will follow.

The Nobel Foundation is very pleased that the intellectual and spiritual message to the world laid down in the laureates' lectures, thanks to the efforts of World Scientific, will reach new readers all over the world.

Lars Gyllensten   *Stig Ramel*
Chairman of the Board   Executive Director

Stockholm, June 1991

PREFACE

The early volumes of the series *Nobel Lectures* were published in 1964–1972. The one covering the Prize in Literature, published in 1969, brought together all the lectures, presentation speeches and laureates' biographies for the period 1901–1967. In 1991, the Nobel Foundation decided to update the series and entrusted me with the editorship in the field of literature.

The two volumes now being published cover the years 1968–1990. For this edition, texts which were previously extant only in languages other than English have been translated, and the biographies have been brought up to date where necessary.

Stockholm, November 1993
Sture Allén
Permanent Secretary of the Swedish Academy

CONTENTS

Literature 1968

YASUNARI KAWABATA

"for his narrative mastery, which with great sensibility expresses the essence of the Japanese mind"

THE NOBEL PRIZE FOR LITERATURE

Speech by ANDERS ÖSTERLING, Ph.D., of the Swedish Academy
Translation

The recipient of this year's Nobel Prize for Literature, the Japanese Yasunari Kawabata, was born in 1899 in the big industrial town of Osaka, where his father was a highly cultured doctor with literary interests. At an early age, however, he was deprived of this favourable growing-up environment on the sudden death of his parents and, as an only child, was sent to his blind and ailing grandfather in a remote part of the country. These tragic losses, doubly significant in view of the Japanese people's intense feeling for blood ties, have undoubtedly affected Kawabata's whole outlook on life and has been one of the reasons for his later study of Buddhist philosophy.

As a student at the imperial university in Tokyo, he decided early on a writing career, and he is an example of the kind of restless absorption that is always a condition of the literary calling. In a youthful short story, which first drew attention to him at the age of twenty-seven, he tells of a student who, during lonely autumn walks on the peninsula of Izu, comes across a poor, despised dancing girl, with whom he has a touching love affair; she opens her pure heart and shows the young man a way to deep and genuine feeling. Like a sad refrain in a folksong the theme recurs with many variations in his following works; he presents his own scale of values and with the years he has won renown far beyond the borders of Japan. True, of his production only three novels and a few short stories have so far been translated into different languages, evidently because translation in this case offers especially great difficulties and is apt to be far too coarse a filter, in which many finer shades of meaning in his richly expressive language must be lost. But the translated works do give us a sufficiently representative picture of his personality.

In common with his older countryman Tanizaki, now deceased, he has admittedly been influenced by modern western realism, but at the same time he has, with greater fidelity, retained his footing in Japan's classical literature and therefore represents a clear tendency to cherish and preserve a genuinely national tradition of style. In Kawabata's narrative art it is still possible to find a sensitively shaded situation poetry which traces its origin back to Murasaki's vast canvas of life and manners in Japan about the year 1000.

Kawabata has been especially praised as a subtle psychologist of women. He has shown his mastery as such in the two short novels "The Snow Kingdom" and "A Thousand Cranes", to use the Swedish titles. In these we see a brilliant capacity to illuminate the erotic episode, an exquisite keenness of observation, a whole network of small, mysterious values, which often put the European narrative technique in the shade. Kawabata's writing is reminiscent of Japanese painting; he is a worshipper of the fragile beauty and melancholy picture language of existence in the life of nature and in man's destiny. If the transience of all outward action can be likened to drifting tufts of grass on the surface of the water, then it is the genuinely Japanese miniature art of haiku poetry which is reflected in Kawabata's prose style.

Even if we feel excluded, as it were, from his writing by a root system, more or less foreign to us, of ancient Japanese ideas and instincts, we may find it tempting in Kawabata to notice certain similarities of temperament with European writers from our own time. Turgeniev is the first to spring to mind, he too is a deeply sensitive story-teller and a broadminded painter of the social scene, with pessimistically coloured sympathies within a time of transition between old and new.

Kawabata's most recent work is also his most outstanding, the novel "Kyoto", completed six years ago and now available in Swedish translation. The story is about the young girl Chiëko, a foundling exposed by her poverty-stricken parents and adopted into the house of the merchant Takichiro, where she is brought up according to old Japanese principles. She is a sensitive, loyal being, who only in secret broods on the riddle of her origin. Popular Japanese belief has it that an exposed child is afflicted with a lifelong curse, in addition to which the condition of being a twin, according to the strange Japanese viewpoint, bears the stigma of shame. One day it happens that she meets a pretty young working girl from a cedar forest near the city and finds that she is her twin sister. They are intimately united beyond the social pale of class—the robust, work-hardened Naëko and the delicate, anxiously guarded Chiëko, but their bewildering likeness soon gives rise to complications and confusion. The whole story is set against the background of the religious festival year in Kyoto from the cherry-blossom spring to the snow-glittering winter.

The city itself is really the leading character, the capital of the old kingdom, once the seat of the mikado and his court, still a romantic sanctuary after a thousand years, the home of the fine arts and elegant handicraft, nowadays exploited by tourism but still a loved place of pilgrimage. With its Shinto and Buddha temples, its old artisan quarters and botanical gardens, the place possesses a poetry which Kawabata expresses in a tender, courteous manner, with no sentimental overtones, but naturally as a moving appeal. He has experienced his country's crushing defeat and no doubt realizes what the future demands in the way of industrial go-ahead spirit, tempo and vitality. But in the post-war wave of violent Americanization his novel is a gentle reminder of the necessity of trying to save something of the old Japan's beauty and individuality for the new. He describes the religious ceremonies in Kyoto with the same meticulous care as he does the textile trade's choice of patterns in the traditional sashes belonging to the women's dresses. These aspects of the novel may have their documentary worth, but the reader prefers to dwell on such a deeply characteristic passage as when the party of middle-class people from the city visits the botanical garden—which has been closed for a long time because the American occupation troops have had their barracks there—in order to see whether the lovely avenue of camphor trees is still intact and able to delight the connoisseur's eye.

With Kawabata, Japan enters the circle of literary Nobel prizewinners for the first time. Essential to the forming of the decision is the fact that, as a writer, he imparts a moral-esthetic cultural awareness with unique artistry, thereby in his way contributing to the spiritual bridge-building between East and West.

Mr Kawabata,

The citation speaks of your narrative mastery, which with great sensibility expresses the essence of the Japanese mind. With great satisfaction we greet you here in our midst today, an honoured guest from afar on this platform. On behalf of the Swedish Academy, I beg to express our hearty congratulations, and at the same time ask you now to receive this year's Nobel Prize for Literature from the hands of His Majesty the King.

YASUNARI KAWABATA

Yasunari Kawabata, son of a highly cultivated physician, was born in 1899 in Osaka. After the early death of his parents he was educated in the country by his maternal grandfather. From 1920 to 1924, Kawabata studied at the Royal University of Tokyo, where he received his degree. He was one of the founders of the publication "Bungai Jidai", the medium of a new movement in modern Japanese literature. Kawabata made his debut as a writer with the short story "Izu dancer", published in 1927. After several distinguished works, the novel "Snow Country" in 1937 secured Kawabata's position as one of the leading authors in Japan. In 1949, the publication of the serials "Thousand Cranes" and "Sound of Mountains" was commenced. He became a member of the Art Academy of Japan in 1953 and four years later he was appointed chairman of the P.E.N. club of Japan. At several international congresses Kawabata was the Japanese delegate for this club. "The Lake" (1955), "The Sleeping Beauty" (1960) and "Kyoto" (1962) belong to his later works and of these novels "Kyoto" is the one that made the deepest impression in the author's native country and abroad. In 1959, Kawabata received the Goethe-medal in Frankfurt.

Yasunari Kawabata died in 1972.

JAPAN, THE BEAUTIFUL AND MYSELF

Nobel lecture, December 12, 1968

by

Yasunari Kawabata

"In the spring, cherry blossoms, in the summer the cuckoo.
In autumn the moon, and in winter the snow, clear, cold."
"The winter moon comes from the clouds to keep me company.
The wind is piercing, the snow is cold."

The first of these poems is by the priest Dōgen (1200—1253) and bears the title "Innate Spirit". The second is by the priest Myōe (1173—1232). When I am asked for specimens of calligraphy, it is these poems that I often choose.

The second poem bears an unusually detailed account of its origins, such as to be an explanation of the heart of its meaning: "On the night of the twelfth day of the twelfth month of the year 1224, the moon was behind clouds. I sat in Zen meditation in the Kakyū Hall. When the hour of the midnight vigil came, I ceased meditation and descended from the hall on the peak to the lower quarters, and as I did so the moon came from the clouds and set the snow to glowing. The moon was my companion, and not even the wolf howling in the valley brought fear. When, presently, I came out of the lower quarters again, the moon was again behind clouds. As the bell was signalling the late-night vigil, I made my way once more to the peak, and the moon saw me on the way. I entered the meditation hall, and the moon, chasing the clouds, was about to sink behind the peak beyond, and it seemed to me that it was keeping me secret company."

There follows the poem I have quoted, and with the explanation that it was composed as Myōe entered the meditation hall after seeing the moon behind the mountain, there comes yet another poem:

"I shall go behind the mountain. Go there too, O moon.
Night after night we shall keep each other company."

Here is the setting for another poem, after Myōe had spent the rest of the night in the meditation hall, or perhaps gone there again before dawn:

"Opening my eyes from my meditations, I saw the moon in the dawn, lighting the window. In a dark place myself, I felt as if my own heart were glowing with light which seemed to be that of the moon:

'My heart shines, a pure expanse of light;
And no doubt the moon will think the light its own.' "

Because of such a spontaneous and innocent stringing together of mere ejaculations as the following, Myōe has been called the poet of the moon:

> "Bright, bright, and bright, bright, bright, and bright, bright.
> Bright and bright, bright, and bright, bright moon."

In his three poems on the winter moon, from late night into the dawn, Myōe follows entirely the bent of Saigyō, another poet-priest, who lived from 1118 to 1190: "Though I compose poetry, I do not think of it as composed poetry." The thirty-one syllables of each poem, honest and straightforward as if he were addressing the moon, are not merely to "the moon as my companion". Seeing the moon, he becomes the moon, the moon seen by him becomes him. He sinks into nature, becomes one with nature. The light of the "clear heart" of the priest, seated in the meditation hall in the darkness before the dawn, becomes for the dawn moon its own light.

As we see from the long introduction to the first of Myōe's poems quoted above, in which the winter moon becomes a companion, the heart of the priest, sunk in meditation upon religion and philosophy, there in the mountain hall, is engaged in a delicate interplay and exchange with the moon; and it is this of which the poet sings. My reason for choosing that first poem when asked for a specimen of my calligraphy has to do with its remarkable gentleness and compassion. Winter moon, going behind the clouds and coming forth again, making bright my footsteps as I go to the meditation hall and descend again, making me unafraid of the wolf: does not the wind sink into you, does not the snow, are you not cold? I choose the poem as a poem of warm, deep, delicate compassion, a poem that has in it the deep quiet of the Japanese spirit. Dr. Yashiro Yukio, internationally known as a scholar of Botticelli, a man of great learning in the art of the past and the present, of the East and the West, has summed up one of the special characteristics of Japanese art in a single poetic sentence: "The time of the snows, of the moon, of the blossoms — — — then more than ever we think of our comrades." When we see the beauty of the snow, when we see the beauty of the full moon, when we see the beauty of the cherries in bloom, when in short we brush against and are awakened by the beauty of the four seasons, it is then that we think most of those close to us, and want them to share the pleasure. The excitement of beauty calls forth strong fellow feelings, yearnings for companionship, and the word "comrade" can be taken to mean "human being". The snow, the moon, the blossoms, words expressive of the seasons as they move one into another, include in the Japanese tradition the beauty of mountains and rivers and grasses and trees, of all the myriad manifestations of nature, of human feelings as well.

That spirit, that feeling for one's comrades in the snow, the moonlight, under the blossoms, is also basic to the tea ceremony. A tea ceremony is a coming together in feeling, a meeting of good comrades in a good season. I may say in passing, that to see my novel *Thousand Cranes* as an evocation of the formal and spiritual beauty of the tea ceremony is a misreading. It is a negative work, and expression of doubt about and warning against the vulgarity into which the tea ceremony has fallen.

> "In the spring, cherry blossoms, in the summer the cuckoo.
> In autumn the full moon, in winter the snow, clear, cold."

One can, if one chooses, see in Dogen's poem the beauty of the four seasons no more than a conventional, ordinary, mediocre stringing together, in a most awkward form of representative images from the four seasons. One can see it as a poem that is not really a poem at all. And yet very similar is the deathbed poem of the priest Ryokan (1758—1831):

> "What shall be my legacy? The blossoms of spring,
> The cuckoo in the hills, the leaves of autumn."

In this poem, as in Dogen's, the commonest of figures and the commonest of words are strung together without hesitation ——— no, to particular effect, rather ——— and so they transmit the very essence of Japan. And it is Ryokan's last poem that I have quoted.

> "A long, misty day in spring:
> I saw it to a close, playing ball with the children."
> "The breeze is fresh, the moon is clear.
> Together let us dance the night away, in what is left of old age."
> "It is not that I wish to have none of the world,
> It is that I am better at the pleasure enjoyed alone."

Ryōkan, who shook off the modern vulgarity of his day, who was immersed in the elegance of earlier centuries, and whose poetry and calligraphy are much admired in Japan today ——— he lived in the spirit of these peoms, a wanderer down country paths, a grass hut for shelter, rags for clothes, farmers to talk to. The profundity of religion and literature was not, for him, in the abstruse. He rather pursued literature and belief in the benign spirit summarized in the Buddhist phrase "a smiling face and gentle words". In his last poem he offered nothing as a legacy. He but hoped that after his death nature would remain beautiful. That could be his bequest. One feels in the poem the emotions of old Japan, and the heart of a religious faith as well.

> "I wondered and wondered when she would come.
> And now we are together. What thoughts need I have?"

Ryōkan wrote love poetry too. This is an example of which I am fond. An old man of sixty-nine (I might point out that at the same age I am the recipient of the Nobel Prize), Ryōkan met a twenty-nine-year-old nun named Teishin, and was blessed with love. The poem can be seen as one of happiness at having met the ageless woman, of happiness at having met the one for whom the wait was so long. The last line is simplicity itself.

Ryōkan died at the age of seventy-three. He was born in the province of Echigo, the present Niigata Prefecture and the setting of my novel *Snow Country*, a northerly region on what is known as the reverse side of Japan, where could winds come down across the Japan Sea from Siberia. He lived his whole life in the snow country, and to his "eyes in their last extremity", when he was old and tired and knew that death was near, and had attained enlightenment, the snow country, as we see in his last poem, was yet more beautiful, I should imagine. I have an essay with the title "Eyes in their Last Extremity".

The title comes from the suicide note of the short-story writer Akutagawa Ryūnosuke (1892—1927). It is the phrase that pulls at me with the greatest strength. Akutagawa said that he seemed to be gradually losing the animal something known as the strength to live, and continued:

"I am living in a world of morbid nerves, clear and cold as ice . . . I do not know when I will summon up the resolve to kill myself. But nature is for me more beautiful than it has ever been before. I have no doubt that you will laugh at the contradiction, for here I love nature even when I am contemplating suicide. But nature is beautiful because it comes to my eyes in their last extremity."

Akutagawa committed suicide in 1927, at the age of thirty-five.

In my essay, *Eyes in their Last Extremity*, I had to say: "How ever alienated one may be from the world, suicide is not a form of enlightenment. However admirable he may be, the man who commits suicide is far from the realm of the saint." I neither admire nor am in sympathy with suicide. I had another friend who died young, an avant-garde painter. He too thought of suicide over the years, and of him I wrote in this same essay: "He seems to have said over and over that there is no art superior to death, that to die is to live," I could see, however, that for him, born in a Buddhist temple and educated in a Buddhist school, the concept of death was very different from that in the West. "Among those who give thoughts to things, is there one who does not think of suicide?" With me was the knowledge that that fellow Ikkyū (1394—1481) twice contemplated suicide. I have "that fellow", because the priest Ikkyū is known even to children as a most amusing person, and because anecdotes about his limitlessly eccentric behavior have come down to us in ample numbers. It is said of him that children climbed his knee to stroke his beard, that wild birds took feed from his hand. It would seem from all this that he was the ultimate in mindlessness, that he was an approachable and gentle sort of priest. As a matter of fact he was the most severe and profound of Zen priests. Said to have been the son of an emperor, he entered a temple at the age of six, and early showed his genius as a poetic prodigy. At the same time he was troubled with the deepest of doubts about religion and life. "If there is a god, let him help me. If there is none, let me throw myself to the bottom of the lake and become food for fishes." Leaving behind these words he sought to throw himself into a lake, but was held back. On another occasion, numbers of his fellows were incriminated when a priest in his Daitokuji Temple committed suicide. Ikkyū went back to the temple, "the burden heavy on my shoulders," and sought to starve himself to death. He gave his collected poetry the title *Collection of the Roiling Clouds,* and himself used the expression "Roiling Clouds" as a pen name. In his collection and its successor are poems quite without parallel in the Chinese and especially the Zen poetry of the Japanese middle ages, erotic poems and poems about the secrets of the bedchamber that leave one in utter astonishment. He sought, by eating fish and drinking spirits and having commerce with women, to go beyond the rules and proscriptions of the Zen of his day, and to seek liberation from them, and thus, turning against established religious forms, he sought in the pursuit of Zen the revival and affirmation of the essence of life, of human existence, in a day civil war and moral collapse.

His temple, the Daitokuji at Murasakino in Kyoto, remains a center of the tea ceremony, and specimens of his calligraphy are greatly admired as hangings in alcoves of tea rooms.

I myself have two specimens of Ikkyū's calligraphy. One of them is a single line: "It is easy to enter the world of the Buddha, it is hard to enter the world of the devil." Much drawn to these words, I frequently make use of them when asked for a specimen of my own calligraphy. They can be read in any number of ways, as difficult as one chooses, but in that world of the devil added to the world of the Buddha, Ikkyū of Zen comes home to me with great immediacy. The fact that for an artist, seeking truth, good, and beauty, the fear and petition even as a prayer in those words about the world of the devil — — — the fact that it should be there apparent on the surface, hidden behind, perhaps speaks with the inevitability of fate. There can be no world of the Buddha without the world of the devil. And the world of the devil is the world difficult of entry. It is not for the weak of heart.

"If you meet a Buddha, kill him. If you meet a patriarch of the law, kill him."

This is a well-known Zen motto. If Buddhism is divided generally into the sects that believe in salvation by faith and those that believe in salvation by one's own efforts, then of course there must be such violent utterances in Zen, which insists upon salvation by one's own efforts. On the other side, the side of salvation by faith, Shinran (1173—1262), the founder of the Shin sect, once said: "The good shall be reborn in paradise, and how much more shall it be so with the bad." This view of things has something in common with Ikkyū's world of the Buddha and world of the devil, and yet at heart the two have their different inclinations. Shinran also said: "I shall not take a single disciple."

"If you meet a Buddha, kill him. If you meet a patriarch of the law, kill him." "I shall not take a single disciple." In these two statements, perhaps, is the rigorous fate of art.

In Zen there is no worship of images. Zen does have images, but in the hall where the regimen of meditation is pursued, there are neither images nor pictures of Buddhas, nor are there scriptures. The Zen disciple sits for long hours silent and motionless, with his eyes closed. Presently he enters a state of impassivity, free from all ideas and all thoughts. He departs from the self and enters the realm of nothingness. This is not the nothingness or the emptiness of the West. It is rather the reverse, a universe of the spirit in which everything communicates freely with everything, transcending bounds, limitless. There are of course masters of Zen, and the disciple is brought toward enlightenment by exchanging questions and answers with his master, and he studies the scriptures. The disciple must, however, always be lord of his own thoughts, and must attain enlightenment through his own efforts. And the emphasis is less upon reason and argument than upon intuition, immediate feeling. Enlightenment comes not from teaching but through the eye awakened inwardly. Truth is in "the discarding of words", it lies "outside words". And so we have the extreme of "silence like thunder", in the Vimalakīrti Nirdeśa Sūtra. Tradition has it that Bodhidharma, a southern Indian prince who lived in about the sixth century and was the founder of Zen in China, sat for nine years in silence facing the wall of a cave, and finally attained enlightenment. The Zen practice of silent meditation in a seated posture derives from Bodhidharma.

Here are two religious poems by Ikkyū:

"Then I ask you answer. When I do not you do not.
What is there then on your heart, O Lord Bodhidharma?"
"And what is it, the heart?
It is the sound of the pine breeze in the ink painting."

Here we have the spirit of Zen in Oriental painting. The heart of the ink painting is in space, abbreviation, what is left undrawn. In the words of the Chinese painter Chin Nung: "You paint the branch well, and you hear the sound of the wind." And the priest Dōgen once more: "Are there not these cases? Enlightenment in the voice of the bamboo. Radiance of heart in the peach blossom."

Ikenobō Sen'ō, a master of flower arranging, once said (the remark is to be found in his Sayings): "With a spray of flowers, a bit of water, one evokes the vastness of rivers and mountains." The Japanese garden too, of course symbolizes the vastness of nature. The Western garden tends to be symmetrical, the Japanese garden asymmetrical, and this is because the asymmetrical has the greater power to symbolize multiplicity and vastness. The asymmetry, of course, rests upon a balance imposed by delicate sensibilities. Nothing is more complicated, varied, attentive to detail, than the Japanese art of landscape gardening. Thus there is the form called the dry landscape, composed entirely of rocks, in which the arrangement of stones gives expression to mountains and rivers that are not present, and even suggests the waves of the great ocean breaking in upon cliffs. Compressed to the ultimate, the Japanese garden becomes the *bonsai* dwarf garden, or the *bonseki*, its dry version.

In the Oriental word for landscape, literally "mountain-water", with its related implications in landscape painting and landscape gardening, there is contained the concept of the sere and wasted, and even of the sad and the threadbare. Yet in the sad, austere, autumnal qualities so valued by the tea ceremony, itself summarized in the expression "gently respectful, cleanly quiet", there lies concealed a great richness of spirit; and the tea room, so rigidly confined and simple, contains boundless space and unlimited elegance. The single flower contains more brightness than a hundred flowers. The great sixteenth-century master of the tea ceremony and flower arranging, Rikyū, taught that it was wrong to use fully opened flowers. Even in the tea ceremony today the general practice is to have in the alcove of the tea room but a single flower, and that a flower in bud. In winter a special flower of winter, let us say a camellia, bearing some such name as White Jewel or Wabisuke, which might be translated literally as "Helpmate in Solitude", is chosen, a camellia remarkable among camellias for its whiteness and the smallness of its blossoms; and but a single bud is set out in the alcove. White is the cleanest of colors, it contains in itself all the other colors. And there must always be dew on the bud. The bud is moistened with a few drops of water. The most splendid of arrangements for the tea ceremony comes in May, when a peony is put out in a celadon vase; but here again there is but a single bud, always with dew upon it. Not only are there drops of water upon the flower, the vase too is frequently moistured.

Among flower vases, the ware that is given the highest rank is old Iga, from the sixteenth and seventeenth centuries, and it commands the highest price. When old Iga has been dampened, its colors and its glow take on a beauty such as to awaken on afresh. Iga was fired at very high temperatures. The straw ash and the smoke from the fuel fell and flowed against the surface, and as the temperature dropped, became a sort of glaze. Because the colors were not fabricated but were rather the result of nature at work in the kiln, color patterns emerged in such varieties as to be called quirks and freaks of the kiln. The rough, austere, strong surfaces of old Iga take on a voluptuous glow when dampened. It breathes to the rhythm of the dew of the flowers.

The taste of the tea ceremony also asks that the tea bowl be moistened before using, to give it its own soft glow.

Ikenobō Sen'ō remarked on another occasion (this too is in his *Sayings*) that "the mountains and strands should appear in their own forms". Bringing a new spirit into his school of flower arranging, therefore, he found "flowers" in broken vessels and withered branches, and in them too the enlightenment that comes from flowers. "The ancients arranged flowers and pursued enlightenment." Here we see how awakening to the heart of the Japanese spirit, under the influence of Zen. And in it too, perhaps, is the heart of a man living in the devastation of long civil wars.

The Tales of Ise, compiled in the tenth century, is the oldest Japanese collection of lyrical episodes, numbers of which might be called short stories. In one of them we learn that the poet Ariwara no Yukihira, having invited guests, put in flowers:

"Being a man of feeling, he had in a large jar a most unusual wistaria. The trailing spray of flowers was upwards of three and a half feet long."

A spray of wistaria of such length is indeed so unusual as to make one have doubts about the credibility of the writer; and yet I can feel in this great spray a symbol of Heian culture. The wistaria is a very Japanese flower, and it has a feminine elegance. Wistaria sprays, as they trail in the breeze, suggest softness, gentleness, reticence. Disappearing and then appearing again in the early summer greenery, they have in them that feeling for the poignant beauty of things long characterized by the Japanese as *mono no aware*. No doubt there was a particular splendor in that spray upwards of three and a half feet long. The splendors of Heian culture a millennium ago and the emergence of a peculiarly Japanese beauty were as wondrous as this "most unusual wistaria", for the culture of T'ang China had at length been absorbed and Japanized. In poetry there came, early in the tenth century, the first of the imperially commissioned anthologies, the *Kokinshū*, and in fiction, the *Tales of Ise*, followed by the supreme masterpieces of classical Japanese prose, the *Tale of Genji* of Lady Murasaki and the *Pillow Book* of Sei Shōnagon, both of whom lived from the late tenth century into the early eleventh. So was established a tradition which influenced and even controlled Japanese literature for eight hundred years. The *Tale of Genji* in particular is the highest pinnacle of Japanese literature. Even down to our day there has not been a piece of fiction to compare with it. That such a modern work should have been written in the eleventh century is a miracle, and as a miracle the work is widely known abroad. Although my grasp of classical Japanese was uncertain, the Heian classics were my principal boyhood reading, and it is the *Genji*, I think, that has meant the most to me. For centuries after it was written, fascination with the *Genji* persisted, and imitations and re-workings did homage to it. The *Genji* was a wide and deep source of nourishment for poetry, of course, and for the fine arts and handicrafts as well, and even for landscape gardening.

Murasaki and Sei Shōnagon, and such famous poets as Izumi Shikibu, who probably died early in the eleventh century, and Akazome Emon, who probably died in the mid-eleventh century, were all ladies-in-waiting in the imperial court. Japanese culture was court culture, and court culture was feminine. The day of the *Genji* and the *Pillow Book* was its finest, when ripeness was moving into decay. One feels in it the sadness at the end of glory, the high tide of Japanese court culture. The court went into its decline, power moved from the court nobility to the military aristocracy, in whose hands it remained through almost seven centuries from the founding of the Kamakura Shogunate in 1192 to the Meiji Restoration in 1867 and 1868. It is not to be thought, however, that either the imperial institution or court culture vanished. In the eighth of the imperial anthologies, the *Shinkokinshū* of the early thirteenth century, the technical dexterity of the *Kokinshū* was pushed yet a step further, and sometimes fell into mere verbal dalliance; but there were added elements of the mysterious, the suggestive, the evocative and inferential elements of sensuous fantasy that have something in common with modern symbolist poetry. Saigyō, who has been mentioned earlier, was a representative poet spanning the two ages, Heian and Kamakura.

> "I dreamt of him because I was thinking of him.
> Had I known it was a dream, I should not have wished to awaken."
> "In my dreams I go to him each night without fail.
> But this is less than a single glimpse in the waking."

These are by Ono no Komachi, the leading poetess of the *Kokinshū,* who sings of dreams, even, with a straightforward realism. But when we come to the following poems of the Empress Eifuku, who lived at about the same time as Ikkyū, in the Muromachi Period, somewhat later than the *Shinko-kinshū,* we have a subtle realism that becomes a melancholy symbolism, delicately Japanese, and seems to me more modern:

> "Shining upon the bamboo thicket where the sparrows twitter,
> The sunlight takes on the color of the autumn."
> "The autumn wind, scattering the bush clover in the garden,
>   sinks into one's bones.
> Upon the wall, the evening sun disappears."

Dōgen, whose poem about the clear, cold snow I have quoted, and Myōe, who wrote of the winter moon as his companion, were of generally the Shinko-kinshū period. Myōe exchanged poems with Saigyō and the two discussed poetry together. The following is from the biography of Myōe by his disciple Kikai:

"Saigyō frequently came and talked of poetry. His own attitude towards poetry, he said, was far from the ordinary. Cherry blossoms, the cuckoo, the moon, snow: confronted with all the manifold forms of nature, his eyes and his ears were filled with emptiness. And were not all the words that came forth true words? When he sang of the blossoms the blossoms were not on his mind, when he sang of the moon he did not think of the moon. As the occasion presented itself, as the urge arose, he wrote poetry. The red rainbow across the sky was as the sky taking on color. The white sunlight was as the sky growing bright. Yet the empty sky, by its nature, was not something to become bright. It was not something to take on color. With a spirit like the empty sky he gives color to all the manifold scenes but not a trace remained. In such poetry was the Buddha, the manifestation of the ultimate truth."

Here we have the emptiness, the nothingness, of the Orient. My own works have been described as works of emptiness, but it is not to be taken for the nihilism of the West. The spiritual foundation would seem to be quite different. Dōgen entitled his poem about the seasons, *Innate Reality,* and even as he sang of the beauty of the seasons he was deeply immersed in Zen.

Literature 1969

SAMUEL BECKETT

*"for his writing, which – in new forms for the novel and drama – in the destitution
of modern man acquires its elevation"*

THE NOBEL PRIZE FOR LITERATURE

Speech by KARL RAGNAR GIEROW, of the Swedish Academy
Translation

Your Majesty, Your Royal Highnesses, Ladies and Gentlemen,
Mix a powerful imagination with a logic in absurdum, and the result will be either a paradox or an Irishman. If it is an Irishman, you will get the paradox into the bargain. Even the Nobel Prize in Literature is sometimes divided. Paradoxically, this has happened in 1969, a single award being addressed to one man, two languages and a third nation, itself divided.

Samuel Beckett was born near Dublin in 1906; as a renowned author he entered the world almost half a century later in Paris when, in the space of three years, five works were published that immediately brought him into the centre of interest: the novel *Molloy* in 1951, its sequel *Malone Meurt* in the same year, the play *En Attendant Godot* in 1952 and in the following year the two novels *L'Innommable*, which concluded the cycle about *Molloy* and *Malone*, and *Watt*.

These dates simply record a sudden appearance. The five works were not new at the time of publication, nor were they written in the order in which they appeared. They had their background in the current situation as well as in Beckett's previous development. The true nature of *Murphy*, a novel from 1938, and the studies of Joyce (1929) and Proust (1931), which illuminate his own initial position, is perhaps most clearly seen in the light of Beckett's subsequent production. For while he has pioneered new modes of expression in fiction and on the stage, Beckett is also allied to tradition, being closely linked not only to Joyce and Proust but to Kafka as well, and the dramatic works from his debut have a heritage from French works of the 1890's and Alfred Jarry's *Ubu Roi*.

In several respects, the novel *Watt* marks a change of phase in this remarkable output. Written in 1942—44 in the South of France—whence Beckett fled from the Nazis, having lived for a long time in Paris—it was to be his last work in English for many years; he made his name in French and did not return to his native tongue for about fifteen years. The world around had also changed when Beckett came to write again after *Watt*. All the other works which made his name were written in the period 1945—49. The Second World War is their foundation; it was after this that his authorship achieved maturity and a message. But these works are not about the war itself, about life at the front or in the French resistance movement (in which Beckett took an active part) but about what happened afterwards, when peace came and the curtain was rent from the unholiest of unholies to reveal the terrifying spectacle of the lengths to which man can go in inhuman degradation—whether ordered or driven by himself—and how much of such degradation man can survive. In this sense the degradation of humanity is a recurrent theme in Beckett's writing and to this extent his philosophy, simply accentuated by elements of the grotesque and of tragic farce, can be described as a negativism that cannot desist from descending to the depths. To the depths it must go because it is only there that pessimistic thought and poetry can work their miracles. What does one get when a negative is printed? A positive, a clarification, with black proving to be the light of day, the parts in deepest shade those which reflect the light source. Its name is fellow-feeling, charity. There are precedents besides the accumulation of abominations in Greek tragedy which led Aristotle to the doctrine of catharsis, purification through horror. Mankind has drawn more strength from Schopenhauer's bitter well than from Schelling's beatific springs, has been more blessed by Pascal's agonized doubt than by Leibniz's blind rational trust in the best of all possible worlds, has reaped—in the field of Irish literature, which has also fed Beckett's writing—a much leaner harvest from the whitewashed clerical pastoral of Oliver Goldsmith than from Dean Swift's vehement denigration of all humankind.

Part of the essence of Beckett's outlook is to be found here—in the difference between an easily-acquired pessimism that rests content with untroubled scepticism and a pessimism that is dearly bought and which penetrates to mankind's utter destitution. The former commences and concludes with the concept that nothing is really of any value, the latter is based on exactly the opposite outlook. For what is worthless cannot be degraded. The perception of human degradation—which we have witnessed perhaps to a greater extent than any previous generation—is not possible if human values are denied. But the experience becomes all the more painful as the recognition of human dignity deepens. This is the source of inner cleansing, the life force nevertheless, in Beckett's pessimism. It houses a love of mankind that grows in understanding as it plumbs further into the depths of abhorrence, a despair that has to reach the utmost bounds of suffering to discover that compassion has no bounds. From that position, in the realms of annihilation, rises the writing of Samuel Beckett like a miserere from all mankind, its muffled minor key sounding liberation to the oppressed and comfort to those in need.

This seems to be stated most clearly in the two masterpieces, *Waiting for Godot* and *Happy Days*, each of which in a way is a development of a biblical text. In the case of *Godot* we have, 'Art thou he that should come, or do we look for another?' The two tramps are confronted with the meaninglessness of existence at its most brutal. It may be a human figure; no laws are as cruel as those of creation and man's peculiar status in creation comes from being the only creature to apply these laws with deliberately evil intent. But if we conceive of a providence—a source even of the immeasurable suffering inflicted by and on mankind—what sort of almighty is it that we—like the tramps—are to meet somewhere, some day? Beckett's answer consists of the title of the play. By the end of the performance, as at the end of our own, we know nothing about this *Godot*. At the final curtain we have no intimation of the force whose progress we have witnessed. But we do know one thing, of which all the horror of this experience cannot deprive us: namely our waiting. This is man's metaphysical predicament of perpetual, uncertain expectation, captured with true poetic simplicity: *En attendant Godot, Waiting for Godot.*

The text for *Happy Days*—"a voice crying in the wilderness"—is more concerned with the predicament of man on earth, of our relationships with one another. In his exposition Beckett has much to say about our capacity for entertaining untroubled illusions in a wilderness void of hope. But this is not the theme. The action simply concerns how isolation, how the sand rises higher and higher until the individual is completely buried in loneliness. Out of the suffocating silence, however, there still rises the head, the voice crying in the wilderness, man's indomitable need to seek out his fellow men right to the end, speak to his peers and find in companionship his solace.

L'Académie Suédoise regrette que Samuel Beckett ne soit pas parmi nous aujourd'hui. Cependant il a choisi pour le représenter l'homme qui le premier a découvert l'importance de l'œuvre maintenant récompensée, son éditeur à Paris M. Jérôme Lindon, et je vous prie, cher Monsieur, de vouloir bien recevoir de la main de Sa Majesté le Roi le Prix Nobel de littérature, décerné par l'Académie à Samuel Beckett.

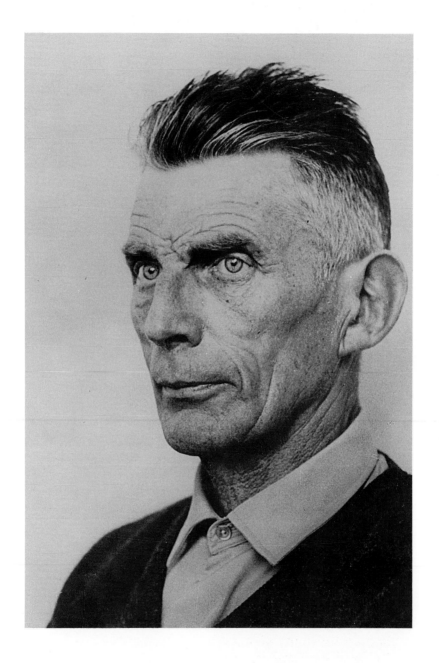

Samuel Beckett

SAMUEL BECKETT

Bio-bibliographic information

1906   Born in Dublin of Irish parents
1927   B.A. Trinity College, Dublin
1928–29 English reader at École Normale Supérieure, Paris
1930   French reader at Trinity College, Dublin
1938   Moved to France
1945   Began writing in French
1989   Died in Paris

Works in French

1951 *Molloy* (novel)
1951 *Malone Meurt* (novel)
1952 *En attendant Godot/Waiting for Godot* (play in two acts)
1953 *L'innommable/The Unnamable* (novel)
1955 *Nouvelles et Textes Pour Rien/Stories and Texts for Nothing*
1957 *Fin de Partie/Endgame* (one-act play) followed by: *Acte sans Paroles I/Act without Words I*
1961 *Comment C'est/How It Is* (novel)
1967 *Têtes Mortes* (*D'un ouvrage abandonné/From an Abandoned Work, Imagination Morte Imaginez/Imagination Dead Imagine, Bing/Ping*)
1970 *Premier amour/First Love* (novel)
1978 *Pas, suivi de Quatre Esquisses/Steps, followed by Four Sketches* (plays)
1979 *Poèmes/Poems*

Works in English

1977 *Ends and Odds: Plays and Sketches*
1979 *All Strange Gone Away* (short prose)
1980 *Company* (short prose)
1980 *The Expelled and other Novellas*
1981 *Rockaby and Other Pieces* (plays and prose)
1982 *Three Occasional Pieces* (plays)
1983 *Worstward Ho* (short prose)
1983 *Disjecta: Miscellaneous Writing and a Dramatic Fragment*
1984 *Collected Shorter Prose 1945–1980*
1986 *Collected Poems 1930–1979*

1989   *Nohow On* (short stories)
1990   *As the Story Was Told: Uncollected and Late Prose*

French translations by the author

1953   *Murphy* (novel)
1957   *Tous Ceux qui Tombent/All that Fall* (radio play)
1960   *La dernière bande/Krapp's Last Tape* (one-act play) followed by *Cendres/Embers* (play)
1963   *Oh Les Beaux Jours/Happy Days* (play in two acts)
1966   *Comédie et Actes Divers/Play and Sundry Acts* (*Comédie/Play, Va-et-Vient/Come and Go, Cascando, Paroles et Musique/Words and Music, Dis Joe/Eh! Joe, Acte sans Paroles II/Act without Words II*)
1968   *Poèmes/Poems*
1969   *Watt* (novel — translated by Ludovic and Agnès Janvier in collaboration with the author)

Works in English translated from French by the author

1972   *The Lost Ones* (short prose)
1973   *First Love* (short prose)
1974   *Mercier and Camier* (novel)
1975   *Malone Dies* (novel)
1975   *The Unnamable* (novel)
1976   *For to End Yet Again and Other Fizzles* (short prose)
1978   *Six Residua* (short prose)
1982   *Ill Seen, Ill Said*

Literature 1970

ALEXANDER SOLZHENITSYN

"for the ethical force with which he has pursued the indispensable traditions of
Russian literature"

THE NOBEL PRIZE FOR LITERATURE
Speech by KARL RAGNAR GIEROW, of the Swedish Academy

Your Majesty, Your Royal Highnesses, Ladies and Gentlemen,

Our passports show where and when we were born, facts that are needed to fix our identity. According to a current theory this also applies to authorship. A literary work belongs to its time and its creator is a product of his social and political situation. There are weighty examples to the contrary but these must be jettisoned or the theory will founder. A case to which it does apply, however, is this year's Nobel Prizewinner in Literature. It is worth emphasizing this because from all points of the compass, not least the West, people are prone for various reasons to make exceptions in his case.

Alexander Solzhenitsyn's passport—I have in mind the one that will convey him to posterity—tells us when and where he was born, details that we need in order to establish his artistic identity. Born in 1918 in Kislovodsk, he belongs to the first generation of Soviet Russian writers who grew up with the new form of government and he is indivisible from the climate and the time in which he was born. Solzhenitsyn himself has said that he cannot contemplate living anywhere but in his native land. His books can; they are already living all round the world, now perhaps more than ever before, in the future perhaps more than now. But their vitality springs not least from the feeling that roots his being to his country and its destiny. Here, too, Solzhenitsyn is of the incomparable Russian tradition. The same background offsets the gigantic predecessors who have derived from Russia's suffering the compelling strength and inextinguishable love that permeate their work. There is little room in their descriptions for idylls according to plan or prescribed information about the future. But it would be a gross misunderstanding of their quest for the truth not to feel in this their profound decisive identification with the country whose life provided their subject matter and for whose life their works are essential. The central figure in this powerful epic is the invincible Mother Russia. She appears in various guises under diverse names. One is Matryona, the main character in one of Solzhenitsyn's stories. Her lined face recalls the constant, indomitable features and re-casts the spell of devotion that she is able to offer and which she so proudly deserves.

Love is blind, the saying goes, and if so, it signifies her instinct for self-preservation. Clear-sighted love does not always conjure up an immediate response. Time and distance may be—and have been—necessary for a true appreciation of the depth and warmth of perceptive feeling. This has not been so in Solzhenitsyn's case. When his novel *One Day in the Life of Ivan Denisovich* first appeared eight years ago, it was recognised at once in his own country and soon all over the world that a major new writer had entered the arena. As Pravda wrote, 'Solzhenitsyn's narrative is reminiscent at times of Tolstoy's artistic force. An unusually talented author has been added to our literature!' It would also be difficult to outdo Pravda's exposé of the power exercised by Solzhenitsyn's narrative art: 'Why is it that our heart contracts with pain as we read this remarkable story at the same time as we feel our spirits soar? The explanation lies in its profound humanity, in the quality of mankind even in the hour of degradation.'

A message about special circumstances seldom travels far and the words that fly round the world are those which appeal to and help us all. Such are the words of Alexander Solzhenitsyn. They speak to us of matters that we need to hear more than ever before, of the individual's indestructible dignity. Wherever that dignity is violated, whatever the reason or the means, his message is not only an accusation but also an assurance: those who commit such a violation are the only ones to be degraded by it. The truth of this is plain to see wherever one travels.

Even the external form which Solzhenitsyn seeks for his work bears witness to his message. This form has been termed the polyphone or horizontal novel. It might equally be described as a story with no chief character. Which is to say that this is not individualism at the expense of the surroundings. But nor may the gallery of persons act as a collective that smothers the individuals of which it is entirely composed. Solzhenitsyn has explained what he means by polyphonism: each person becomes the chief character whenever the action concerns him. This is not just a technique, it is a creed. The narrative focuses on the only human element in existence, the human individual, with equal status among equals, one destiny among millions and a million destinies in one. This is the whole of humanism in a nutshell, for the kernel is love of mankind. This year's Nobel Prize for Literature has been awarded to the proclaimer of such a humanism.

THE NOBEL PRIZE FOR LITERATURE 1970

Address to ALEXANDER SOLZHENITSYN BY KARL RAGNAR GIEROW, of the Swedish Academy, on December 10, 1974

Not only for the Swedish Academy but for all of us the ceremony today has its particular significance: we can, finally, hand over to the laureate of 1970 the insignia of his award.

Mr Alexander Solzhenitsyn: I have already made two speeches to you. The first one you couldn't listen to, because there was a frontier to cross. The second one I couldn't deliver, because there was a frontier to cross. Your presence here today doesn't mean that the frontiers have at last been abolished. On the contrary, it means that you are now on this side of a border that still exists. But the spirit of your writings, as I understand it, the driving force of your work, like the spirit and force of Alfred Nobel's last will and testament, is to open all frontiers, to enable man to meet man, freely and confidently.

The difficulty is that such a confidence can only be built on truth. And nowhere in this world of ours is truth always greeted with pure pleasure. Truth goes from house to house, and the dog barks at whom he does not know, says a stern old philosopher. But all the more happy and grateful are those who recognize the wandering stranger and ask him to spend the night and his life with them, in the deep, even desperate hope that the day may not be far off when a frontier is, as it should be, merely a line on the map, which we pass on our way to friends. Such should be, and could be, the case all around the prospering and tormented planet which we inhabit.

Alexander Solzhenitsyn, my dear friend, with these few words I convey to you the warm congratulations of the Swedish Academy and ask you to receive from the hands of His Majesty the King the insignia of the prize to whose value you have added your honour.

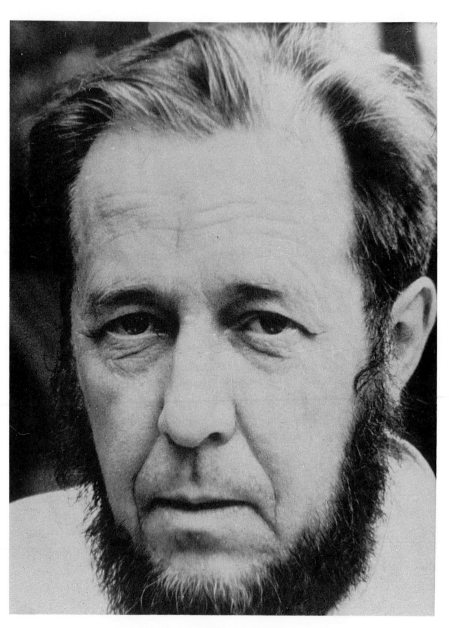

A. SOLZHENITSYN
Translation

I was born at Kislovodsk on 11th December, 1918. My father had studied philological subjects at Moscow University, but did not complete his studies, as he enlisted as a volunteer when war broke out in 1914. He became an artillery officer on the German front, fought throughout the war and died in the summer of 1918, six months before I was born. I was brought up by my mother, who worked as a shorthand-typist, in the town of Rostov on the Don, where I spent the whole of my childhood and youth, leaving the grammar school there in 1936. Even as a child, without any prompting from others, I wanted to be a writer and indeed I turned out a good deal of the usual juvenilia. In the 1930's, I tried to get my writings published but I could not find anyone willing to accept my manuscripts. I wanted to acquire a literary education but in Rostov such an education that would suit my wishes was not to be obtained. To move to Moscow was not possible, partly because my mother was alone and in poor health and partly because of our modest circumstances. I therefore began to study at the Department of Mathematics at Rostov University, where it proved that I had a considerable aptitude for mathematics. But although I found it easy to learn this subject I did not feel that I wished to devote my whole life to it. Nevertheless, it was to play a beneficial role in my destiny later on and on at least two occasions it rescued me from death. For I would probably not have survived the eight years in camps if I had not, as a mathematician, been transferred to a so-called *sharashka*, where I spent four years; and later, during my exile, I was allowed to teach mathematics and physics, which helped to ease my existence and made it possible for me to write. If I had had a literary education it is quite likely that I should not have survived these ordeals but would instead have been subjected to even greater pressures. Later on, it is true, I began to get some literary education as well; this was from 1939 to 1941, during which time, along with university studies in physics and mathematics, I also studied by correspondence at the Institute of History, Philosophy and Literature in Moscow.

In 1941, a few days before the outbreak of the war, I graduated from the Department of Physics and Mathematics at Rostov University. At the beginning of the war, owing to weak health, I was detailed to serve as a driver of horsedrawn vehicles during the winter of 1941—1942. Later, because of my mathematical knowledge, I was transferred to an artillery school, from which after a crash course I passed out in November 1942. Immediately after this I was put in command of an artillery position-finding company and in this capacity served without a break right in the front line until I was arrested in February 1945. This happened in East Prussia, a region which is linked with my destiny in a remarkable way. As early as 1937, as a first-year student, I chose to write a descriptive essay on "The Samsonov Disaster" of 1914 in East Prussia and studied material on this; and in 1945 I myself went to this area (at the time of writing, autumn 1970, the book *August 1914* has just been completed).

I was arrested on the grounds of what the censorship had found during the years 1944—45 in my correspondence with a school friend, mainly because of certain disrespectful remarks about Stalin, although we referred to him in disguised terms. As a further basis for the "charge" there were used the drafts of stories and reflections which had been found in my map case. These, however, were not sufficient for a "prosecution" and in July 1945 I was "sentenced" in my absence, in accordance with a procedure then frequently applied, after a resolution by the OSO (the Special Committee of the NKVD), to eight years in a detention camp (at that time this was considered a mild sentence).

I served the first part of my sentence in several correctional work camps of mixed types (this kind of camp is described in the play *The Tenderfoot and the Tramp*). In 1946, as a mathematician, I was transferred to the group of scientific research institutes of the MVD—MGB*. I spent the middle period of my sentence in such "SPECIAL PRISONS" (*The First Circle*). In 1950 I was sent to the newly established Special Camps which were intended only for political prisoners. In such a camp in the town of Ekibastuz in Kazakhstan (*One Day in the Life of Ivan Deni-sovich*), I worked as a miner, a bricklayer and a foundryman. There I contracted a tumour which was operated on, but the condition was not cured (its character was not established until later on).

One month after I had served the full term of my eight-year sentence, there came, without any new judgement and even without a "resolution from the OSO", an administrative decision to the effect that I was not to be released but EXILED FOR LIFE to Kok-Terek (southern Kazakhstan).

* Ministry of Internal Affairs, Ministry of State Security.

This measure was not directed specially against me but was a very usual procedure at that time. I served this exile from March 1953 (on March 5th, when Stalin's death was made public, I was allowed for the first time to go out without an escort) until June 1956. Here my cancer had developed rapidly and at the end of 1953, I was very near death. I was unable to eat, I could not sleep and was severely affected by the poisons from the tumour. However, I was able to go to a cancer clinic at Tashkent, where, during 1954, I was cured (*The Cancer Ward, Right Hand*). During all the years of exile I taught mathematics and physics in a primary school and during my hard and lonely existence I wrote prose in secret (in the camp I could only write down poetry from memory). I managed, however, to keep what I had written and to take it with me to the European part of the country, where in the same way I continued, as far as the outer world was concerned, to occupy myself with teaching and, in secret, to devote myself to writing, at first in the Vladimir district (*Matryona's Farm*) and afterwards in Ryazan.

During all the years until 1961, not only was I CONVINCED that I should never see a single line of mine in print in my lifetime but also I scarcely dared allow any of my close acquaintances to read anything I had written because I feared that this would become known. Finally, at the age of 42, this secret authorship began to wear me down. The most difficult thing of all to bear was that I could not get my works judged by people with literary training. In 1961, after the 22nd Congress of the U.S.S.R. Communist Party and Tvardovsky's speech at this, I decided to emerge and to offer *One Day in the Life of Ivan Denisovich.*

Such an emergence seemed then to me, and not without reason, to be very risky because it might lead to the loss of my manuscripts and to my own destruction. But on that occasion things turned out successfully and after protracted efforts, A. T. Tvardovsky was able to print my novel one year later. The printing of my work was, however, stopped almost immediately and the authorities stopped both my plays and (in 1964) the novel, *The First Circle,* which in 1965 was seized together with my papers from the past years. During these months it seemed to me that I had committed an unpardonable mistake by revealing my work prematurely and that because of this I should not be able to carry it to a conclusion.

It is almost always impossible to evaluate at the time events which you have already experienced and to understand their meaning with the guidance of their effects. All the more unpredictable and surprising to us will be the course of future events.

A. SOLZHENITSYN
NOBEL LECTURE in Literature 1970*

1

Just as that puzzled savage who has picked up—a strange cast-up from the ocean?—something unearthed from the sands?—or an obscure object fallen down from the sky?—intricate in curves, it gleams first dully and then with a bright thrust of light. Just as he turns it this way and that, turns it over, trying to discover what to do with it, trying to discover some mundane function within his own grasp, never dreaming of its higher function.

So also we, holding Art in our hands, confidently consider ourselves to be its masters; boldly we direct it, we renew, reform and manifest it; we sell it for money, use it to please those in power; turn to it at one moment for amusement—right down to popular songs and night-clubs, and at another—grabbing the nearest weapon, cork or cudgel—for the passing needs of politics and for narrow-minded social ends. But art is not defiled by our efforts, neither does it thereby depart from its true nature, but on each occasion and in each application it gives to us a part of its secret inner light.

But shall we ever grasp the whole of that light? Who will dare to say that he has DEFINED Art, enumerated all its facets? Perhaps once upon a time someone understood and told us, but we could not remain satisfied with that for long; we listened, and neglected, and threw it out there and then, hurrying as always to exchange even the very best—if only for something new! And when we are told again the old truth, we shall not even remember that we once possessed it.

One artist sees himself as the creator of an independent spiritual world; he hoists onto his shoulders the task of creating this world, of peopling it and of bearing the all-embracing responsibility for it; but he crumples beneath it, for a mortal genius is not capable of bearing such a burden. Just as man in general, having declared himself the centre of existence, has not succeeded in creating a balanced spiritual system. And if misfortune overtakes him, he casts the blame upon the age-long disharmony of the world, upon the complexity of today's ruptured soul, or upon the stupidity of the public.

Another artist, recognizing a higher power above, gladly works as a humble apprentice beneath God's heaven; then, however, his responsbility for everything that is written or drawn, for the souls which perceive his work, is more exacting than ever. But, in return, it is not he who has created this world, not he who directs it, there is no doubt as to its foundations; the artist has merely to be more keenly aware than others of the harmony of the world, of the beauty and ugliness of the human contribution to it, and to communicate this acutely to his fellow-men. And in misfortune, and even at the depths of existence—in

*Delivered only to the Swedish Academy and not actually given as a lecture.

destitution, in prison, in sickness—his sense of stable harmony never deserts him.

But all the irrationality of art, its dazzling turns, its unpredictable discoveries, its shattering influence on human beings—they are too full of magic to be exhausted by this artist's vision of the world, by his artistic conception or by the work of his unworthy fingers.

Archeologists have not discovered stages of human existence so early that they were without art. Right back in the early morning twilights of mankind we received it from Hands which we were too slow to discern. And we were too slow to ask: FOR WHAT PURPOSE have we been given this gift? What are we to do with it?

And they were mistaken, and will always be mistaken, who prophesy that art will disintegrate, that it will outlive its forms and die. It is we who shall die—art will remain. And shall we comprehend, even on the day of our destruction, all its facets and all its possibilities?

Not everything assumes a name. Some things lead beyond words. Art inflames even a frozen, darkened soul to a high spiritual experience. Through art we are sometimes visited—dimly, briefly—by revelations such as cannot be produced by rational thinking.

Like that little looking-glass from the fairy-tales: look into it and you will see—not yourself—but for one second, the Inaccessible, whither no man can ride, no man fly. And only the soul gives a groan . . .

2

One day Dostoevsky threw out the enigmatic remark: "Beauty will save the world". What sort of a statement is that? For a long time I considered it mere words. How could that be possible? When in bloodthirsty history did beauty ever save anyone from anything? Ennobled, uplifted, yes—but whom has it saved?

There is, however, a certain peculiarity in the essence of beauty, a peculiarity in the status of art: namely, the convincingness of a true work of art is completely irrefutable and it forces even an opposing heart to surrender. It is possible to compose an outwardly smooth and elegant political speech, a headstrong article, a social program, or a philosophical system on the basis of both a mistake and a lie. What is hidden, what distorted, will not immediately become obvious.

Then a contradictory speech, article, program, a differently constructed philosophy rallies in opposition—and all just as elegant and smooth, and once again it works. Which is why such things are both trusted and mistrusted.

In vain to reiterate what does not reach the heart.

But a work of art bears within itself its own verification: conceptions which are devised or stretched do not stand being portrayed in images, they all come crashing down, appear sickly and pale, convince no one. But those works of art which have scooped up the truth and presented it to us as a living force— they take hold of us, compel us, and nobody ever, not even in ages to come, will appear to refute them.

So perhaps that ancient trinity of Truth, Goodness and Beauty is not simply an empty, faded formula as we thought in the days of our self-confident, materialistic youth? If the tops of these three trees converge, as the scholars maintained, but the too blatant, too direct stems of Truth and Goodness are crushed, cut down, not allowed through—then perhaps the fantastic, unpredictable, unexpected stems of Beauty will push through and soar TO THAT VERY SAME PLACE, and in so doing will fulfil the work of all three?

In that case Dostoevsky's remark, "Beauty will save the world", was not a careless phrase but a prophecy? After all HE was granted to see much, a man of fantastic illumination.

And in that case art, literature might really be able to help the world today?

It is the small insight which, over the years, I have succeeded in gaining into this matter that I shall attempt to lay before you here today.

3

In order to mount this platform from which the Nobel lecture is read, a platform offered to far from every writer and only once in a lifetime, I have climbed not three or four makeshift steps, but hundreds and even thousands of them; unyielding, precipitous, frozen steps, leading out of the darkness and cold where it was my fate to survive, while others—perhaps with a greater gift and stronger than I—have perished. Of them, I myself met but a few on the Archipelago of GULag,* shattered into its fractionary multitude of islands; and beneath the millstone of shadowing and mistrust I did not talk to them all, of some I only heard, of others still I only guessed. Those who fell into that abyss already bearing a literary name are at least known, but how many were never recognized, never once mentioned in public? And virtually no one managed to return. A whole national literature remained there, cast into oblivion not only without a grave, but without even underclothes, naked, with a number tagged on to its toe. Russian literature did not cease for a moment, but from the outside it appeared a wasteland! Where a peaceful forest could have grown, there remained, after all the felling, two or three trees overlooked by chance.

And as I stand here today, accompanied by the shadows of the fallen, with bowed head allowing others who were worthy before to pass ahead of me to this place, as I stand here, how am I to divine and to express what THEY would have wished to say?

This obligation has long weighed upon us, and we have understood it. In the words of Vladimir Solov'ev:

> Even in chains we ourselves must complete
> That circle which the gods have mapped out for us.

Frequently, in painful camp seethings, in a column of prisoners, when chains

* The Central Administration of Corrective Labour Camps.

of lanterns pierced the gloom of the evening frosts, there would well up inside us the words that we should like to cry out to the whole world, if the whole world could hear one of us. Then it seemed so clear: what our successful ambassador would say, and how the world would immediately respond with its comment. Our horizon embraced quite distinctly both physical things and spiritual movements, and it saw no lop-sidedness in the indivisible world. These ideas did not come from books, neither were they imported for the sake of coherence. They were formed in conversations with people now dead, in prison cells and by forest fires, they were tested against THAT life, they grew out of THAT existence.

When at last the outer pressure grew a little weaker, my and our horizon broadened and gradually, albeit through a minute chink, we saw and knew "the whole world". And to our amazement the whole world was not at all as we had expected, as we had hoped; that is to say a world living "not by that", a world leading "not there", a world which could exclaim at the sight of a muddy swamp, "what a delightful little puddle!", at concrete neck stocks, "what an exquisite necklace!"; but instead a world where some weep inconsolate tears and others dance to a light-hearted musical.

How could this happen? Why the yawning gap? Were we insensitive? Was the world insensitive? Or is it due to language differences? Why is it that people are not able to hear each other's every distinct utterance? Words cease to sound and run away like water—without taste, colour, smell. Without trace.

As I have come to understand this, so through the years has changed and changed again the structure, content and tone of my potential speech. The speech I give today.

And it has little in common with its original plan, conceived on frosty camp evenings.

4

From time immemorial man has been made in such a way that his vision of the world, so long as it has not been instilled under hypnosis, his motivations and scale of values, his actions and intentions are determined by his personal and group experience of life. As the Russian saying goes, "Do not believe your brother, believe your own crooked eye." And that is the most sound basis for an understanding of the world around us and of human conduct in it. And during the long epochs when our world lay spread out in mystery and wilderness, before it became encroached by common lines of communication, before it was transformed into a single, convulsively pulsating lump—men, relying on experience, ruled without mishap within their limited areas, within their communities, within their societies, and finally on their national territories. At that time it was possible for individual human beings to perceive and accept a general scale of values, to distinguish between what is considered normal, what incredible; what is cruel and what lies beyond the boundaries of wickedness; what is honesty, what deceit. And although the scattered peoples led extremely different lives and their social values were often strikingly at odds, just as their systems of weights and measures did not agree, still these discrepancies surprised only occasional travellers, were reported in journals under the name of wonders, and bore no danger to mankind which was not yet one.

But now during the past few decades, imperceptibly, suddenly, mankind has become one—hopefully one and dangerously one—so that the concussions and inflammations of one of its parts are almost instantaneously passed on to others, sometimes lacking in any kind of necessary immunity. Mankind has become one, but not steadfastly one as communities or even nations used to be; not united through years of mutual experience, neither through possession of a single eye, affectionately called crooked, nor yet through a common native language, but, surpassing all barriers, through international broadcasting and print. An avalanche of events descends upon us—in one minute half the world hears of their splash. But the yardstick by which to measure those events and to evaluate them in accordance with the laws of unfamiliar parts of the world— this is not and cannot be conveyed via soundwaves and in newspaper columns. For these yardsticks were matured and assimilated over too many years of too specific conditions in individual countries and societies; they cannot be exchanged in mid-air. In the various parts of the world men apply their own hard-earned values to events, and they judge stubbornly, confidently, only according to their own scales of values and never according to any others.

And if there are not many such different scales of values in the world, there are at least several; one for evaluating events near at hand, another for events far away; aging societies possess one, young societies another; unsuccessful people one, successful people another. The divergent scales of values scream in discordance, they dazzle and daze us, and in order that it might not be painful we steer clear of all other values, as though from insanity, as though from illusion, and we confidently judge the whole world according to our own home values. Which is why we take for the greater, more painful and less bearable disaster not that which is in fact greater, more painful and less bearable, but that which lies closest to us. Everything which is further away, which does not threaten this very day to invade our threshold—with all its groans, its stifled cries, its destroyed lives, even if it involves millions of victims—this we consider on the whole to be perfectly bearable and of tolerable proportions.

In one part of the world, not so long ago, under persecutions not inferior to those of the ancient Romans', hundreds of thousands of silent Christians gave up their lives for their belief in God. In the other hemisphere a certain madman, (and no doubt he is not alone), speeds across the ocean to DELIV-ER us from religion—with a thrust of steel into the high priest! He has calculated for each and every one of us according to his personal scale of values!

That which from a distance, according to one scale of values, appears as enviable and flourishing freedom, at close quarters, and according to other values, is felt to be infuriating constraint calling for buses to be overthrown. That which in one part of the world might represent a dream of incredible prosperity, in another has the exasperating effect of wild exploitation demanding immediate strike. There are different scales of values for natural catastrophes: a flood craving two hundred thousand lives seems less significant than our local accident. There are different scales of values for personal insults: sometimes even an ironic smile or a dismissive gesture is humiliating, while for others cruel beatings are forgiven as an unfortunate joke. There are different scales of values for punishment and wickedness: according to one, a month's arrest, banishment to the country, or an isolation-cell where one is fed on white rolls and milk, shatters the imagination and fills the newspaper columns with rage. While according to another, prison sentences of twenty-five years, isolation-cells where the walls are covered with ice and the prisoners stripped to their underclothes, lunatic asylums for the sane, and countless unreasonable people who for some reason will keep running away, shot on the frontiers—all this is common and accepted. While the mind is especially at peace concerning that exotic part of the world about which we know virtually nothing, from which we do not even receive news of events, but only the trivial, out-of-date guesses of a few correspondents.

Yet we cannot reproach human vision for this duality, for this dumbfounded incomprehension of another man's distant grief, man is just made that way. But for the whole of mankind, compressed into a single lump, such mutual incomprehension presents the threat of imminent and violent destruction. One world, one mankind cannot exist in the face of six, four or even two scales of values: we shall be torn apart by this disparity of rhythm, this disparity of vibrations.

A man with two hearts is not for this world, neither shall we be able to live side by side on one Earth.

5

But who will co-ordinate these value scales, and how? Who will create for mankind one system of interpretation, valid for good and evil deeds, for the unbearable and the bearable, as they are differentiated today? Who will make clear to mankind what is really heavy and intolerable and what only grazes the skin locally? Who will direct the anger to that which is most terrible and not to that which is nearer? Who might succeed in transferring such an understanding beyond the limits of his own human experience? Who might succeed in impressing upon a bigoted, stubborn human creature the distant joy and grief of others, an understanding of dimensions and deceptions which he himself has never experienced? Propaganda, constraint, scientific proof—all are useless. But fortunately there does exist such a means in our world! That means is art. That means is literature.

They can perform a miracle: they can overcome man's detrimental peculiarity of learning only from personal experience so that the experience of other people passes him by in vain. From man to man, as he completes his brief spell on Earth, art transfers the whole weight of an unfamiliar, lifelong experience with all its burdens, its colours, its sap of life; it recreates in the flesh an unknown experience and allows us to possess it as our own.

And even more, much more than that; both countries and whole continents repeat each other's mistakes with time lapses which can amount to centuries. Then, one would think, it would all be so obvious! But no; that which some nations have already experienced, considered and rejected, is suddenly discovered by others to be the latest word. And here again, the only substitute for an experience we ourselves have never lived through is art, literature. They possess a wonderful ability: beyond distinctions of language, custom, social structure, they can convey the life experience of one whole nation to another. To an inexperienced nation they can convey a harsh national trial lasting many decades, at best sparing an entire nation from a superfluous, or mistaken, or even disastrous course, thereby curtailing the meanderings of human history.

It is this great and noble property of art that I urgently recall to you today from the Nobel tribune.

And literature conveys irrefutable condensed experience in yet another invaluable direction; namely, from generation to generation. Thus it becomes the living memory of the nation. Thus it preserves and kindles within itself the flame of her spent history, in a form which is safe from deformation and slander. In this way literature, together with language, protects the soul of the nation.

(In recent times it has been fashionable to talk of the levelling out of nations, of the disappearance of different races in the melting-pot of contemporary civilization. I do not agree with this opinion, but its discussion remains another question. Here it is merely fitting to say that the disappearance of nations would have impoverished us no less than if all men had become alike, with one personality and one face. Nations are the wealth of mankind, its collective personalities; the very least of them wears its own special colours and bears within itself a special facet of divine intention.)

But woe to that nation whose literature is disturbed by the intervention of power. Because that is not just a violation against "freedom of print", it is the closing down of the heart of the nation, a slashing to pieces of its memory. The nation ceases to be mindful of itself, it is deprived of its spiritual unity, and despite a supposedly common language, compatriots suddenly cease to understand one another. Silent generations grow old and die without ever having talked about themselves, either to each other or to their descendants. When writers such as Achmatova and Zamjatin—interred alive throughout their lives—are condemned to create in silence until they die, never hearing the echo of their written words, then that is not only their personal tragedy, but a sorrow to the whole nation, a danger to the whole nation.

In some cases moreover—when as a result of such a silence the whole of history ceases to be understood in its entirety— it is a danger to the whole of mankind.

6

At various times and in various countries there have arisen heated, angry and exquisite debates as to whether art and the artist should be free to live for themselves, or whether they should be for ever mindful of their duty towards society and serve it albeit in an unprejudiced way. For me there is no dilemma, but I shall refrain from raising once again the train of arguments. One of the most brilliant addresses on this subject was actually Albert Camus' Nobel speech, and I would happily subscribe to his conclusions. Indeed, Russian literature has for several decades manifested an inclination not to become too lost in contemplation of itself, not to flutter about too frivolously. I am not ashamed to continue this tradition to the best of my ability. Russian literature has long been familiar with the notions that a writer can do much within his society, and that it is his duty to do so.

Let us not violate the RIGHT of the artist to express exclusively his own experiences and introspections, disregarding everything that happens in the world beyond. Let us not DEMAND of the artist, but—reproach, beg, urge and entice him—that we may be allowed to do. After all, only in part does he himself develop his talent; the greater part of it is blown into him at birth as a finished product, and the gift of talent imposes responsibility on his free will. Let us assume that the artist does not OWE anybody anything· nevertheless, it is painful to see how, by retiring into his self-made worlds or the spaces of his subjective whims, he CAN surrender the real world into the hands of men who are mercenary, if not worthless, if not insane.

Our Twentieth Century has proved to be more cruel than preceding centuries, and the first fifty years have not erased all its horrors. Our world is rent asunder by those same old cave-age emotions of greed, envy, lack of control, mutual hostility which have picked up in passing respectable pseudonyms like class struggle, racial conflict, struggle of the masses, trade-union disputes. The primeval refusal to accept a compromise has been turned into a theoretical principle and is considered the virtue of orthodoxy. It demands millions of sacrifices in ceaseless civil wars, it drums into our souls that there is no such thing as unchanging, universal concepts of goodness and justice, that they are all fluctuating and inconstant. Therefore the rule—always do what's most profitable to your party. Any professional group no sooner sees a convenient opportunity to BREAK OFF A PIECE, even if it be unearned, even if it be superfluous, than it breaks it off there and then and no matter if the whole of society comes tumbling down. As seen from the outside, the amplitude of the tossings of western society is approaching that point beyond which the system becomes metastable and must fall. Violence, less and less embarrassed by the limits imposed by centuries of lawfulness, is brazenly and victoriously striding across the whole world, unconcerned that its infertility has been demonstrated and proved many times in history. What is more, it is not simply crude power that triumphs abroad, but its exultant justification. The world is being inundated by the brazen conviction that power can do anything, justice nothing. Dostoevsky's DEVILS—apparently a provincial nightmare fantasy of the last century—are crawling across the whole world in front of our very eyes, infesting countries where they could not have been dreamed of; and by means of the hijackings, kidnappings, explosions and fires of recent years they are announcing their determination to shake and destroy civilization! And they may well succeed. The young, at an age when they have not yet any experience other than sexual, when they do not yet have years of personal suffering and personal understanding behind them, are jubilantly repeating our depraved Russian blunders of the Nineteenth Century, under the impression that they are discovering something new. They acclaim the latest wretched degradation on the part of the Chinese Red Guards as a joyous example. In shallow lack of understanding of the age-old essence of mankind, in the naive confidence of inexperienced hearts they cry: let us drive away THOSE cruel, greedy oppressors, governments, and the new ones (we!), having laid aside grenades and rifles, will be just and understanding. Far from it! ... But of those who have lived more and understand, those who could oppose these young—many do not dare oppose, they even suck up, anything not to appear "conservative". Another Russian phenomenon of the Nineteenth Century which Dostoevsky called SLAVERY TO PROGRESSIVE QUIRKS.

The spirit of Munich has by no means retreated into the past; it was not merely a brief episode. I even venture to say that the spirit of Munich prevails in the Twentieth Century. The timid civilized world has found nothing with which to oppose the onslaught of a sudden revival of barefaced barbarity, other than concessions and smiles. The spirit of Munich is a sickness of the will of successful people, it is the daily condition of those who have given themselves up to the thirst after prosperity at any price, to material well-being as the chief goal of earthly existence. Such people—and there are many in today's world—elect passivity and retreat, just so as their accustomed life might drag on a bit longer, just so as not to step over the threshold of hardship today—and tomorrow, you'll see, it will all be all right. (But it will never be all right! The price of cowardice will only be evil; we shall reap courage and victory only when we dare to make sacrifices.)

And on top of this we are threatened by destruction in the fact that the physically compressed, strained world is not allowed to blend spiritually; the molecules of knowledge and sympathy are not allowed to jump over from one half to the other. This presents a rampant danger: THE SUPPRESSION OF INFORMATION between the parts of the planet. Contemporary science knows that suppression of information leads to entropy and total destruction. Suppression of information renders international signatures and agreements illusory; within a muffled zone it costs nothing to reinterpret any agreement, even simpler—to forget it, as though it had never really existed. (Orwell understood this supremely.) A muffled zone is, as it were, populated not by inhabitants of the Earth, but by an expeditionary corps from Mars; the people know nothing intelligent about the rest of the Earth and are prepared to go and trample it down in the holy conviction that they come as "liberators".

A quarter of a century ago, in the great hopes of mankind, the United Nations Organization was born. Alas, in an immoral world, this too grew up to be immoral. It is not a United Nations Organization but a United Governments Organization where all governments stand equal; those which are freely elected, those imposed forcibly, and those which have seized power with weapons. Relying on the mercenary partiality of the majority UNO jealously guards the freedom of some nations and neglects the freedom of others. As a result of an obedient vote it declined to undertake the investigation of private appeals—the groans, screams and beseechings of humble individual PLAIN PEOPLE—not large enough a catch for such a great organization. UNO made no effort to make the Declaration of Human Rights, its best document in twenty-five years, into an OBLIGATORY condition of membership confronting the governments. Thus it betrayed those humble people into the will of the governments which they had not chosen.

It would seem that the appearance of the contemporary world rests solely in the hands of the scientists; all mankind's technical steps are determined by them. It would seem that it is precisely on the international goodwill of scientists, and not of politicians, that the direction of the world should depend. All the more so since the example of the few shows how much could be achieved were they all to pull together. But no; scientists have not manifested any clear attempt to become an important, independently active force of mankind. They spend entire congresses in renouncing the sufferings of others; better to stay safely within the precincts of science. That same spirit of Munich has spread above them its enfeebling wings.

What then is the place and role of the writer in this cruel, dynamic, split world on the brink of its ten destructions? After all we have nothing to do with letting off rockets, we do not even push the lowliest of hand-carts, we are quite scorned by those who respect only material power. Is it not natural for us too to step back, to lose faith in the steadfastness of goodness, in the indivisibility of truth, and to just impart to the world our bitter, detached observations: how mankind has become hopelessly corrupt, how men have degenerated, and how difficult it is for the few beautiful and refined souls to live amongst them?

But we have not even recourse to this flight. Anyone who has once taken up the WORD can never again evade it; a writer is not the detached judge of his compatriots and contemporaries, he is an accomplice to all the evil committed in his native land or by his countrymen. And if the tanks of his fatherland have flooded the asphalt of a foreign capital with blood, then the brown spots have slapped against the face of the writer forever. And if one fatal night they suffocated his sleeping, trusting Friend, then the palms of the writer bear the bruises from that rope. And if his young fellow citizens breezily declare the superiority of depravity over honest work, if they give themselves over to drugs or seize hostages, then their stink mingles with the breath of the writer.

Shall we have the temerity to declare that we are not responsible for the sores of the present-day world?

7

However, I am cheered by a vital awareness of WORLD LITERATURE as of a single huge heart, beating out the cares and troubles of our world, albeit presented and perceived differently in each of its corners.

Apart from age-old national literatures there existed, even in past ages, the conception of world literature as an anthology skirting the heights of the national literatures, and as the sum total of mutual literary influences. But there occured a lapse in time: readers and writers became acquainted with writers of other tongues only after a time lapse, sometimes lasting centuries, so that mutual influences were also delayed and the anthology of national literary heights was revealed only in the eyes of descendants, not of contemporaries.

But today, between the writers of one country and the writers and readers of another, there is a reciprocity if not instantaneous then almost so. I experience this with myself. Those of my books which, alas, have not been printed in my own country have soon found a responsive, worldwide audience, despite hurried and often bad translations. Such distinguished western writers as Heinrich Böll have undertaken critical analysis of them. All these last years, when my work and freedom have not come crashing down, when contrary to the laws of gravity they have hung suspended as though on air, as though on NOTHING—on the invisible dumb tension of a sympathetic public membrane; then it was with grateful warmth, and quite unexpectedly for myself, that I learnt of the further support of the international brotherhood of writers. On my fiftieth birthday I was astonished to receive congratulations from well-known western writers. No pressure on me came to pass by unnoticed. During my dangerous weeks of exclusion from the Writers' Union the WALL OF DEFENCE advanced by the world's prominent writers protected me from worse persecutions; and Norwegian writers and artists hospitably prepared a roof for me, in the event of my threatened exile being put into effect. Finally even the advancement of my name for the Nobel Prize was raised not in the country where I live and write, but by François Mauriac and his colleagues. And later still entire national writers' unions have expressed their support for me.

Thus I have understood and felt that world literature is no longer an abstract anthology, nor a generalization invented by literary historians; it is rather a certain common body and a common spirit, a living heartfelt unity reflecting the growing unity of mankind. State frontiers still turn crimson, heated by electric wire and bursts of machine fire; and various ministries of internal affairs still think that literature too is an "internal affair" falling under their jurisdiction; newspaper headlines still display: "No right to interfere in our internal affairs!" Whereas there are no INTERNAL AFFAIRS left on our crowded Earth! And mankind's sole salvation lies in everyone making everything his business; in the people of the East being vitally concerned with what is thought in the West, the people of the West vitally concerned with what goes on in the East. And literature, as one of the most sensitive, responsive instruments possessed by the human creature, has been one of the first to adopt, to assimilate, to catch hold of this feeling of a growing unity of mankind. And so I turn with confidence to the world literature of today— to hundreds of friends whom I have never met in the flesh and whom I may never see.

Friends! Let *us* try to help if we are worth anything at all! Who from time immemorial has constituted the uniting, not the dividing, strength in your countries, lacerated by discordant parties, movements, casts and groups? There in its essence is the position of writers: expressers of their native language— the chief binding force of the nation, of the very earth its people occupy, and at best of its national spirit.

I believe that world literature has it in its power to help mankind, in these its troubled hours, to see itself as it really is, notwithstanding the indoctrinations of prejudiced people and parties. World literature has it in its power to convey condensed experience from one land to another so that we might cease to be split and dazzled, that the different scales of values might be made to agree, and one nation learn correctly and concisely the true history of another with such strength of recognition and painful awareness as it had itself experienced the same, and thus might it be spared from repeating the same cruel mistakes. And perhaps under such conditions we artists will be able to cultivate within ourselves a field of vision to embrace the WHOLE WORLD: in the centre observing like any other human being that which lies nearby, at the edges we shall begin to draw in that which is happening in the rest of the world. And we shall correlate, and we shall observe world proportions.

And who, if not writers, are to pass judgement—not only on their unsuccessful governments, (in some states this is the easiest way to earn one's bread, the occupation of any man who is not lazy), but also on the people themselves, in their cowardly humiliation or self-satisfied weakness? Who is to pass judgement on the light-weight sprints of youth, and on the young pirates brandishing their knives?

We shall be told: what can literature possibly do against the ruthless onslaught of open violence? But let us not forget that violence does not live alone and is not capable of living alone: it is necessarily interwoven with falsehood. Between them lies the most intimate, the deepest of natural bonds. Violence finds its only refuge in falsehood, falsehood its only support in violence. Any man who has once acclaimed violence as his METHOD must inexorably choose falsehood as his PRINCIPLE. At its birth violence acts openly and even with pride. But no sooner does it become strong, firmly established, than it senses the rarefaction of the air around it and it cannot continue to exist without descending into a fog of lies, clothing them in sweet talk. It does not always, not necessarily, openly throttle the throat, more often it demands from its subjects only an oath of allegiance to falsehood, only complicity in falsehood.

And the simple step of a simple courageous man is not to partake in falsehood, not to support false actions! Let THAT enter the world, let it even reign in the world—but not with my help. But writers and artists can achieve more: they can CONQUER FALSEHOOD! In the struggle with falsehood art always did win and it always does win! Openly, irrefutably for everyone! Falsehood can hold out against much in this world, but not against art.

And no sooner will falsehood be dispersed than the nakedness of violence will be revealed in all its ugliness—and violence, decrepit, will fall.

That is why, my friends, I believe that we are able to help the world in its white-hot hour. Not by making the excuse of possessing no weapons, and not by giving ourselves over to a frivolous life—but by going to war!

Proverbs about truth are well-loved in Russian. They give steady and sometimes striking expression to the not inconsiderable harsh national experience:

ONE WORD OF TRUTH SHALL OUTWEIGH THE WHOLE WORLD.

And it is here, on an imaginary fantasy, a breach of the principle of the conservation of mass and energy, that I base both my own activity and my appeal to the writers of the whole world.

Literature 1971

PABLO NERUDA

"for a poetry that with the action of an elemental force brings alive a continent's destiny and dreams"

THE NOBEL PRIZE FOR LITERATURE

Speech by KARL RAGNAR GIEROW, of the Swedish Academy
Translation

Your Majesty, Your Royal Highnesses, Ladies and Gentlemen,

No great writer gains lustre from a Nobel Prize. It is the Nobel Prize that gains lustre from the recipient—provided the right one has been chosen. But who is the right one? According to Nobel's will, as we have just heard, the prize is to reward work in "an ideal direction". This is not pure Swedish. One may work under conditions that are not ideal. One can, according to the presumption made by Oscar Wilde, be an ideal husband. The word ideal simply indicates something that corresponds to reasonable expectations. But that is not enough for a Nobel prize. In Nobel's time the word still had philosophical connotations as well. By ideal was meant something which only exists in one's imagination, never in the world of the senses. This is perhaps true of the ideal husband, but not of the ideal Nobel prize winner.

The spirit of Nobel's will tells us what he had in mind. The contribution must be one which will benefit mankind. But any work of art worthy of the name does this, so does any literary work with a serious purpose, and so far that matter does that which aims at nothing more serious than raising a healthy laugh. The clause in the will has so much to say that it leaves us without a clear message. One of the few cases, however, where it does take on a definite meaning is this year's winner of the Nobel Prize for Literature: Pablo Neruda. His work benefits mankind precisely because of its direction. It is my impossible task here to indicate this in a few words. To sum up, Neruda is like catching a condor with a butterfly net. Neruda, in a nutshell, is an unreasonable proposition: the kernel bursts the shell.

Nevertheless, one can do something to describe this kernel. What Neruda has achieved in his writing is community with existence. This sounds simple, and is perhaps our most difficult problem. He himself, in one of his *New Elemental Odes,* has defined it in the formula: harmony with Man and the Earth. The direction in his work, the direction which can so justly be called ideal, is indicated by the path which has brought him to this harmony. His starting point was isolation and dissonance.

So it was in the love poems of his youth. What these *Twenty Poems of Love and One Ode of Desperation* depict is the meeting between two people's desolation in the shadow of destruction, and in the next major work, *Residence on Earth,* he is still "alone among shifting matter".

The turning point was reached in Spain. It was as if a release from the shadow of death and a way towards fellowship were opened when he saw friends and fellow writers taken away in fetters and executed. He found the fellowship of the oppressed and persecuted. He found it when he returned from the Spain of the Civil War to his own country, the battleground for conquistadors over the centuries. But out of the fellowship with this territory of terror there grew, too, awareness of its riches, pride over its past, and hope for its future, for that which he saw shimmering like a mirage far to the East. With this, Neruda's work was transformed into the poetry of political and social preparedness under the banner of redress and visions of the future—not least so in *Canto general,* partly written while in exile in his own country for no other offence than an opinion. The opinion was that his country belonged to him and his compatriots and that no man's dignity should be insulted.

This huge collection is no more than a drop in Neruda's brimming output. In his work a continent awakens to consciousness. To require moderation in such an inspiration is as if to demand system and order from a jungle and restraint from a volcano.

The fact that Neruda's *œuvre* is so difficult to view as a whole may also make it difficult to recognize what distances he has put behind him. One of his later collections of poems is called *Estravagario*. The word seems to be a new one and comprises both extravagance and vagabondage, whim and errantry. For the way from *Canto general* was still long and full of experiences, enriching or bitter. The territory of terror was found to lie in more than one part of the globe and Neruda saw this with the indignation of one who feels himself duped. The erstwhile idol who was set up everywhere in "the stucco statutes of a moustachioed god in boots" now appeared in an ever more merciless light, as did the similarity in methods and trappings between the two leader figures whom he called just Moustache and Little Moustache. But at the same time Neruda was also led to a new relationship to Love and to Woman, to the origin and continuance of life, perhaps most beautifully expressed in yet another masterpiece from recent years, *La Barcarola*. Whither Neruda's path will take him now, it is not for anyone to say. But the direction is the one already set, harmony with Man and the Earth, and we shall follow with high expectations this remarkable poetry, which with the overflowing vitality of an awakening continent resembles one of its rivers, growing all the mightier and more majestic the closer it approaches the estuary and the sea.

Cher Maître,

Votre Estravagario vous a mené loin à travers des pays et des époques. Une fois il vous a mené vers une cité minière où les mineurs avaient peint un hommage sur cette terre qui est vraiment la vôtre. Il disait : Bienvenue à Neruda. C'étaient les mots de la dignité humaine opprimée à celui qui était son porte-parole. Votre tour du monde vous a aujourd'hui mené ici : dans la ville aux clochers vert-de-grisés que vous chantâtes une fois. Et je répète le même hommage : Bienvenido Neruda. Avec lui je transmets aussi les félicitations de l'Académie suédoise et vous prie maintenant de recevoir des mains de Sa Majesté le Roi le Prix Nobel de littérature de cette année.

PABLO NERUDA

Pablo Neruda, whose real name is Neftalí Ricardo Reyes Basoalto, was born on 12 July, 1904, in the town of Parral in Chile. His father was a railway employee and his mother, who died shortly after his birth, a teacher. Some years later his father, who had then moved to the town of Temuco, remarried doña Trinidad Candia Malverde. The poet spent his childhood and youth in Temuco, where he also got to know Gabriela Mistral, head of the girls' secondary school, who took a liking to him. At the early age of thirteen he began to contribute some articles to the daily "La Mañana", among them *Entusiasmo y Perseverancia* — his first publication — and his first poem. In 1920, he became a contributor to the literary journal "Selva Austral" under the pen name of Pablo Neruda, which he adopted in memory of the Czechoslovak poet Jan Neruda (1834—1891). Some of the poems Neruda wrote at that time are to be found in his first published book: *Crepusculario* (1923). The following year saw the publication of *Veinte poemas de amor y una canción desesperada*, one of his best-known and most translated works. Alongside his literary activities, Neruda studied French and pedagogy at the University of Chile in Santiago.

Between 1927 and 1935, the government put him in charge of a number of honorary consulships, which took him to Burma, Ceylon, Java, Singapore, Buenos Aires, Barcelona, and Madrid. His poetic production during that difficult period included, among other works, the collection of esoteric surrealistic poems *Residencia en la tierra* (1933), which marked his literary breakthrough.

The Spanish Civil War and the murder of García Lorca, whom Neruda knew, affected him strongly and made him join the Republican movement, first in Spain and later in France, where he started working on his collection of poems *España en el Corazón* (1937). The same year he returned to his native country, to which he had been recalled, and his poetry during the following period was characterised by an orientation towards political and social matters. *España en el Corazón* had a great impact by virtue of its being printed in the middle of the front during the Civil War.

In 1939, Neruda was appointed consul for the Spanish emigration, residing in Paris, and, shortly afterwards, Consul General in Mexico, where he rewrote his *Canto General de Chile*, transforming it into an epic poem about the whole South American continent, its nature, its people and its historical destiny. This work, entitled *Canto General*, was published the same year in Mexico, and also underground in Chile.

It consists of approximately 250 poems brought together into fifteen literary cycles and constitutes the central part of Neruda's production. Shortly after its publication, *Canto General* was translated into some ten languages. Nearly all these poems were created in a difficult situation, when Neruda was living abroad.

In 1943, Neruda returned to Chile and in 1945 he was elected senator of the Republic, also joining the Communist Party of Chile. Due to his protests against President González Videla's repressive policy against striking miners in 1947, he had to live underground in his own country for two years until he managed to leave in 1949. After living in different European countries he returned home in 1952. A great deal of what he published during that period bears the stamp of his political activities; one example is *Las Uvas y el Viento* (1954), which can be regarded as the diary of Neruda's exile. In *Odas elementales* (1954 — 1959) his message is expanded into a more extensive description of the world, where the objects of the hymns — things, events and relations — are duly presented in alphabetic form.

Neruda's production is exceptionally extensive. For example, his *Obras Completas*, constantly re-published, comprised 459 pages in 1951; in 1962 the number of pages was 1,925 and in 1968 it amounted to 3,237, in two volumes. Among his works of the last few years can be mentioned *Cien sonetos de amor* (1959), which includes poems dedicated to his wife Matilde Urrutia, *Memorial de Isla Negra*, a poetic work of an autobiographic character in five volumes, published on the occasion of his sixtieth birthday, *Arte de pajáros* (1966), *La Barcarola* (1967), the play *Fulgor y muerte de Joaquín Murieta* (1967), *Las manos del día* (1968), *Fin del mundo* (1969), *Las piedras del cielo* (1970), and *La espada encendida*.

Further works:

Geografía infructuosa/Barren Geography (poetry), 1972
El mar y las campanas/The Sea and the Bells, tr. (poetry), 1973
Incitación al nixonicidio y alabanza de la revolución chilena/A Call for the Destruction of Nixon and Praise for the Chilean Revolution, tr. (poetry), 1974
El corazón amarillo/The Yellow Heart (poetry), 1974
Defectos escogidos/Selected Waste Paper (poetry), 1974
Elegía/Elegy (poetry), 1974
Confieso que he vivido. Memorias/Memoirs, tr. (prose), 1974
Para nacer he nacido/Passions and Impressions, tr. (prose), 1978

Pablo Neruda died in 1973.

TOWARDS THE SPLENDID CITY

by

PABLO NERUDA

Chile

Nobel Lecture, December 13, 1971

Translation

My speech is going to be a long journey, a trip that I have taken through regions that are distant and antipodean, but not for that reason any less similar to the landscape and the solitude in Scandinavia. I refer to the way in which my country stretches down to the extreme South. So remote are we Chileans that our boundaries almost touch the South Pole, recalling the geography of Sweden, whose head reaches the snowy northern region of this planet.

Down there on those vast expanses in my native country, where I was taken by events which have already fallen into oblivion, one has to cross, and I was compelled to cross, the Andes to find the frontier of my country with Argentina. Great forests make these inaccessible areas like a tunnel through which our journey was secret and forbidden, with only the faintest signs to show us the way. There were no tracks and no paths, and I and my four companions, riding on horseback, pressed forward on our tortuous way, avoiding the obstacles set by huge trees, impassable rivers, immense cliffs and desolate expanses of snow, blindly seeking the quarter in which my own liberty lay. Those who were with me knew how to make their way forward between the dense leaves of the forest, but to feel safer they marked their route by slashing with their machetes here and there in the bark of the great trees, leaving tracks which they would follow back when they had left me alone with my destiny.

Each of us made his way forward filled with this limitless solitude, with the green and white silence of trees and huge trailing plants and layers of soil laid down over centuries, among half-fallen tree trunks which suddenly appeared as fresh obstacles to bar our progress. We were in a dazzling and secret world of nature which at the same time was a growing menace of cold, snow and persecution. Everything became one: the solitude, the danger, the silence, and the urgency of my mission.

Sometimes we followed a very faint trail, perhaps left by smugglers or ordinary criminals in flight, and we did not know whether many of them had perished, surprised by the icy hands of winter, by the fearful snowstorms which suddenly rage in the Andes and engulf the traveller, burying him under a whiteness seven storeys high.

On either side of the trail I could observe in the wild desolation something which betrayed human activity. There were piled up branches which had lasted out many winters, offerings made by hundreds who had journeyed there, crude burial mounds in memory of the fallen, so that the passer should think of those who had not been able to struggle on but had remained there under the snow for ever. My comrades, too, hacked off with their machetes branches which brushed our heads and bent down over us from the colossal trees, from oaks whose last leaves were scattering before the winter storms. And I too left a tribute at every mound, a visiting card of wood, a branch from the forest to deck one or other of the graves of these unknown travellers.

We had to cross a river. Up on the Andean summits there run small streams which cast themselves down with dizzy and insane force, forming waterfalls that stir up earth and stones with the violence they bring with them from the heights. But this time we found calm water, a wide mirror-like expanse which could be forded. The horses splashed in, lost their foothold and began to swim towards the other bank. Soon my horse was almost completely covered by the water, I began to plunge up and down without support, my feet fighting desperately while the horse struggled to keep its head above water. Then we got across. And hardly we reached the further bank when the seasoned countryfolk with me asked me with scarce-concealed smiles:

"Were you frightened?"

"Very. I thought my last hour had come", I said.

"We were behind you with our lassoes in our hands", they answered.

"Just there", added one of them, "my father fell and was swept away by the current. That didn't happen to you."

We continued till we came to a natural tunnel which perhaps had been bored through the imposing rocks by some mighty vanished river or created by some tremor of the earth when these heights had been formed, a channel that we entered where it had been carved out in the rock in granite. After only a few steps our horses began to slip when they sought for a foothold in the uneven surfaces of the stone and their legs were bent, sparks flying from beneath their iron shoes—several times I expected to find myself thrown off and lying there on the rock. My horse was bleeding from its muzzle and from its legs, but we persevered and continued on the long and difficult but magnificent path.

There was something awaiting us in the midst of this wild primeval forest. Suddenly, as if in a strange vision, we came to a beautiful little meadow huddled among the rocks: clear water, green grass, wild flowers, the purling of brooks and the blue heaven above, a generous stream of light unimpeded by leaves.

There we stopped as if within a magic circle, as if guests within some hallowed place, and the ceremony I now took part in had still more the air of something sacred. The cowherds dismounted from their horses. In the midst of the space, set up as if in a rite, was the skull of an ox. In silence the men approached it one after the other and put coins and food in the eyesockets of the skull. I joined them in this sacrifice intended for stray travellers, all kinds of refugees who would find bread and succour in the dead ox's eye sockets.

But the unforgettable ceremony did not end there. My country friends took off their hats and began a strange dance, hopping on one foot around the abandoned skull, moving in the ring of footprints left behind by the many others who had passed there before them. Dimly I understood, there by the side of my inscrutable companions, that there was a kind of link between unknown people, a care, an appeal and an answer even in the most distant and isolated solitude of this world.

Further on, just before we reached the frontier which was to divide me from my native land for many years, we came at night to the last pass between the mountains. Suddenly we saw the glow of a fire as a sure sign of a human presence, and when we came nearer we found some half-ruined buildings, poor hovels which seemed to have been abandoned. We went into one of them and saw the glow of fire from tree trunks burning in the middle of the floor, carcasses of huge trees, which burnt there day and night and from which came smoke that made its way up through the cracks in the roof and rose up like a deep-blue veil in the midst of the darkness. We saw mountains of stacked cheeses, which are made by the people in these high regions. Near the fire lay a number of men grouped like sacks. In the silence we could distinguish the notes of a guitar and words in a song which was born of the embers and the darkness, and which carried with it the first human voice we had encountered during our journey. It was a song of love and distance, a cry of love and longing for the distant spring, from the towns we were coming away from, for life in its limitless extent. These men did not know who we were, they knew nothing about our flight, they had never heard either my name or my poetry; or perhaps they did, perhaps they knew us? What actually happened was that at this fire we sang and we ate, and then in the darkness we went into some primitive rooms. Through them flowed a warm stream, volcanic water in which we bathed, warmth which welled out from the mountain chain and received us in its bosom.

Happily we splashed about, dug ourselves out, as it were, liberated ourselves from the weight of the long journey on horseback. We felt refreshed, reborn, baptised, when in the dawn we started on the journey of a few miles which was to eclipse me from my native land. We rode away on our horses singing, filled with a new air, with a force that cast us out on to the world's broad highway which awaited me. This I remember well, that when we sought to give the mountain dwellers a few coins in gratitude for their songs, for the food, for the warm water, for giving us lodging and beds, I would rather say for the unexpected heavenly refuge that had met us on our journey, our offering was rejected out of hand. They had been at our service, nothing more. In this taciturn "nothing" there were hidden things that were understood, perhaps a recognition, perhaps the same kind of dreams.

Ladies and Gentlemen,

I did not learn from books any recipe for writing a poem, and I, in my turn, will avoid giving any advice on mode or style which might give the new poets even a drop of supposed insight. When I am recounting in this speech something about past events, when reliving on this occasion a never-forgotten occurrence, in this place which is so different from what that was, it is because in the course of my life I have always found somewhere the necessary support, the formula which had been waiting for me not in order to be petrified in my words but in order to explain me to myself.

During this long journey I found the necessary components for the making of the poem. There I received contributions from the earth and from the soul. And I believe that poetry is an action, ephemeral or solemn, in which there enter as equal partners solitude and solidarity, emotion and action, the nearness to oneself, the nearness to mankind and to the secret manifestations of nature. And no less strongly I think that all this is sustained —man and his shadow, man and his conduct, man and his poetry—by an ever-wider sense of community, by an effort which will for ever bring together the reality and the dreams in us because it is precisely in this way that poetry unites and mingles them. And therefore I say that I do not know, after so many years, whether the lessons I learned when I crossed a daunting river, when I danced around the skull of an ox, when I bathed my body in the cleansing water from the topmost heights—I do not know whether these lessons welled forth from me in order to be imparted to many others or whether it was all a message which was sent to me by others as a demand or an accusation. I do not know whether I experienced this or created it, I do not know whether it was truth or poetry, something passing or permanent, the poems I experienced in this hour, the experiences which I later put into verse.

From all this, my friends, there arises an insight which the poet must learn through other people. There is no insurmountable solitude. All paths lead to the same goal: to convey to others what we are. And we must pass through solitude and difficulty, isolation and silence in order to reach forth to the enchanted place where we can dance our clumsy dance and sing our sorrowful song—but in this dance or in this song there are fulfilled the most ancient rites of our conscience in the awareness of being human and of believing in a common destiny.

The truth is that even if some or many consider me to be a sectarian, barred from taking a place at the common table of friendship and responsibility, I do not wish to defend myself, for I believe that neither accusation nor defence is among the tasks of the poet. When all is said, there is no individual poet who administers poetry, and if a poet sets himself up to accuse his fellows or if some other poet wastes his life in defending himself against reasonable or unreasonable charges, it is my conviction that only vanity can so mislead us. I consider the enemies of poetry to be found not among those who practise poetry or guard it but in mere lack of agreement in the poet. For this reason no poet has any considerable enemy other than his own incapacity to make himself understood by the most forgotten and exploited of his contemporaries, and this applies to all epochs and in all countries.

The poet is not a "little god". No, he is not a "little god". He is not picked out by a mystical destiny in preference to those who follow other crafts and professions. I have often maintained that the best poet is he who prepares our daily bread: the nearest baker who does not imagine himself to be a god. He does his majestic and unpretentious work of kneading the dough, consigning it to the oven, baking it in golden colours and handing us our daily bread as a duty of fellowship. And, if the poet succeeds in achieving this simple consciousness, this too will be transformed into an element in an immense activity, in a simple or complicated structure which constitutes the building of a community, the changing of the conditions which surround mankind, the handing over of mankind's products: bread, truth, wine, dreams. If the poet joins this never-completed struggle to extend to the hands of each and all his part of his undertaking, his effort and his tenderness to the daily work of all people, then the poet must take part, the poet will take part, in the sweat, in the bread, in the wine, in the whole dream of humanity. Only in this indispensable way of being ordinary people shall we give back to poetry the mighty breadth which has been pared away from it little by little in every epoch, just as we ourselves have been whittled down in every epoch.

The mistakes which led me to a relative truth and the truths which repeatedly led me back to the mistakes did not allow me—and I never made any claims to it—to find my way to lead, to learn what is called the creative process, to reach the heights of literature that are so difficult of access. But one thing I realized—that it is we ourselves who call forth the spirits through our own myth-making. From the matter we use, or wish to use, there arise later on obstacles to our own development and the future development. We are led infallibly to reality and realism, that is to say to become indirectly conscious of everything that surrounds us and of the ways of change, and then we see, when it seems to be late, that we have erected such an exaggerated barrier that we are killing what is alive instead of helping life to develop and blossom. We force upon ourselves a realism which later proves to be more burdensome than the bricks of the building, without having erected the building which we had regarded as an indispensable part of our task. And, in the contrary case, if we succeed in creating the fetish of the incomprehensible (or the fetish of that which is comprehensible only to a few), the fetish of the exclusive and the secret, if we exclude reality and its realistic degenerations, then we find ourselves suddenly surrounded by an impossible country, a quagmire of leaves, of mud, of cloud, where our feet sink in and we are stifled by the impossibility of communicating.

As far as we in particular are concerned, we writers within the tremendously far-flung American region, we listen unceasingly to the call to fill this mighty void with beings of flesh and blood. We are conscious of our duty as fulfillers—at the same time we are faced with the unavoidable task of critical communication within a world which is empty and is not less full of unjustices, punishments and sufferings because it is empty—and we feel also the responsibility for reawakening the old dreams which sleep in statues of stone in the ruined ancient monuments, in the wide-stretching silence in planetary plains, in dense primeval forests, in rivers which roar like thunder. We must fill with words the most distant places in a dumb continent and we are intoxicated by this task of making fables and giving names. This is perhaps what is decisive in my own humble case, and if so my exaggerations or my abundance or my rhetoric would not be anything other than the simplest of events within the daily work of an American. Each and every one of my verses has chosen to take its place as a tangible object, each and every one of my poems has claimed to be a useful working instrument, each and every one of my songs has endeavoured to serve as a sign in space for a meeting between paths which cross one another, or as a piece of stone or wood on which someone, some others, those who follow after, will be able to carve the new signs.

By extending to these extreme consequences the poet's duty, in truth or in error, I determined that my posture within the community and before life should be that of in a humble way taking sides. I decided this when I saw so many honourable misfortunes, lone victories, splendid defeats. In the midst of the arena of America's struggles I saw that my human task was none other than to join the extensive forces of the organized masses of the people, to join with life and soul with suffering and hope, because it is only from this great popular stream that the necessary changes can arise for the authors and for the nations. And even if my attitude gave and still gives rise to bitter or friendly objections, the truth is that I can find no other way for an author in our far-flung and cruel countries, if we want the darkness to blossom, if we are concerned that the millions of people who have learnt neither to read us nor to read at all, who still cannot write or write to us, are to feel at home in the area of dignity without which it is impossible for them to be complete human beings.

We have inherited this damaged life of peoples dragging behind them the burden of the condemnation of centuries, the most paradisaical of peoples, the purest, those who with stones and metals made marvellous towers, jewels of dazzling brilliance—peoples who were suddenly despoiled and silenced in the fearful epochs of colonialism which still linger on.

Our original guiding stars are struggle and hope. But there is no such thing as a lone struggle, no such thing as a lone hope. In every human being are combined the most distant epochs, passivity, mistakes, sufferings, the pressing urgencies of our own time, the pace of history. But what would have become of me if, for example, I had contributed in some way to the maintenance of the feudal past of the great American continent? How should I then have been able to raise my brow, illuminated by the honour which Sweden has conferred on me, if I had not been able to feel some pride in having taken part, even to a small extent, in the change which has now come over my country? It is necessary to look at the map of America, to place oneself before its splendid multiplicity, before the cosmic generosity of the wide places which surround us, in order to understand why many writers refuse to share the dishonour and plundering of the past, of all that which dark gods have taken away from the American peoples.

I chose the difficult way of divided responsibility and, rather than to repeat the worship of the individual as the sun and centre of the system, I have preferred to offer my services in all modesty to an honourable army which may from time to time commit mistakes but which moves forward unceasingly and struggles every day against the anachronism of the refractory and the impatience of the opinionated. For I believe that my duties as a poet involve friendship not only with the rose and with symmetry, with exalted love and endless longing, but also with unrelenting human occupations which I have incorporated into my poetry.

It is today exactly one hundred years since an unhappy and brilliant poet, the most awesome of all despairing souls, wrote down this prophecy: "A l'aurore, armés d'une ardente patience, nous entrerons aux splendides Villes." "In the dawn, armed with a burning patience, we shall enter the splendid Cities."

I believe in this prophecy of Rimbaud, the Visionary. I come from a dark region, from a land separated from all others by the steep contours of its geography. I was the most forlorn of poets and my poetry was provincial, oppressed and rainy. But always I had put my trust in man. I never lost hope. It is perhaps because of this that I have reached as far as I now have with my poetry and also with my banner.

Lastly, I wish to say to the people of good will, to the workers, to the poets, that the whole future has been expressed in this line by Rimbaud: only with a *burning patience* can we conquer the splendid City which will give light, justice and dignity to all mankind.

In this way the song will not have been sung in vain.

Literature 1972

HEINRICH BÖLL

"for his writing which through its combination of a broad perspective on his time and a sensitive skill in characterization has contributed to a renewal of German literature"

THE NOBEL PRIZE FOR LITERATURE

Speech by KARL RAGNAR GIEROW, Permanent Secretary of the Swedish
Academy
Translation from the Swedish text

Your Royal Highnesses, Ladies and Gentlemen,
He who attempts to seize in a single grasp the bountiful and very varied
authorship of Heinrich Böll finds himself holding an abstraction. Through
these writings—begun twenty years ago and culminating in last year's novel
Gruppenbild mit Dame — there runs, however, a twin theme that might serve
as such a synoptic abstraction. This could be phrased: The homeless and the
aesthetics of the humane. But Böll's homeless are not ill-fated individuals or
human wreckage cast up outside the bulwarks of society. He tells of a society
without a roof over its head, a derailed, displaced epoch, standing on every
street corner with hand outstretched, begging for the charity of a kindred spirit
and human fellowship. This is the situation underlying Böll's *Ästhetik des
Humanen*.

He writes about what every human being seeks in order to lead a human
life, in little things as in great, about "das Wohnen, die Nachbarschaft und die
Heimat, das Geld und die Liebe, Religion und Mahlzeiten", to quote his own
enumeration. With its whole register from satire and high-spirited parody to
deep suffering, this is a form of passionately engaged aesthetics and it also contains his literary program. He who sets out to portray the bare necessities of life
keeps both feet on the ground.

Yet Böll has declared "Ich brauche wenig Wirklichkeit", a word to note,
coming from one who is regarded and who perhaps regards himself as a
realistic narrator. The reality he needs so little is that of the classic 19th century novel, the reality that after a meticulous study of detail is faithfully
reproduced. Böll is highly proficient at the method but employs it ironically;
there is no limit to the superfluity of detail.

But the jesting with this conscientious form of registration is itself a demon-
stration of how little Böll needs such a reality. His mastery includes the ability
to bring his setting and its figures to life with scanty, sometimes barely sug-
gested lines.

There is however another reality which Böll's writing continually requires:
the background to his existence, the air his generation breathed, the heritage
into which it came. That reality is the recurrent, intrusively observed subject
of Heinrich Böll's writing, from the start up to the magnum opus already mentioned, *Gruppenbild mit Dame*, which so far crowns his work. Böll's real breakthrough came in the years 1953, 1954 and 1955 with three novels published
one after the other — *Und sagte kein einziges Wort; Haus ohne Hüter,* and *Das
Brot der frühen Jahre.* Although it was presumably not the author's intention,

these three titles serve to indicate the reality which he so persistently and force-fully depicts. His background was Germany's years of famine, it was *Das Brot der frühen Jahre,* the bread that never sufficed and often was not there, the bread that had to be begged for or stolen if one was to survive, and that diet is an indelible memory. The heritage which he and his contemporaries had to administer was *Haus ohne Hüter,* house without caretaker, an existence in ruins, with time a widow and the future fatherless. The air he and his contemporaries breathed was inhaled with the heavy hand of dictatorship on their throats, *Und sagte kein einziges Wort,* because the hand smothered every sound.

It is not the smallest German miracle that after such years of destitution a new generation of writers, thinkers and researchers was ready so soon to shoulder their country's and their own essential task in the spiritual life of our time. The renewal of German literature, to which Heinrich Böll's achievements witness and of which they are a significant part, is not an experiment with form—a drowning man scorns the butterfly stroke. Instead it is a rebirth out of annihilation, a resurrection, a culture which, ravaged by icy nights and condemned to extinction, sends up new shoots, blossoms and matures to the joy and benefit of us all. Such was the kind of work Alfred Nobel wished his Prize to reward.

Dear Mr. Böll,

As a given consequence of the homelessness that is one of the main themes of your writing, comes the striving that you yourself have indicated with the words: "Die Suche nach einer bewohnbaren Sprache in einem bewohnbaren Land". This implies an antithesis of homelessness, a writing in which everyone can feel at home. You reject a literature for an initiated circle, you have declared, adding significantly: "Eine Kirche wird eingeweiht, aber durch diesen Akt der Einweihung nicht geschlossen, sondern geöffnet". It is this openness for the human aspect which gives space and raises the arches higher in your works. And it is works in that spirit which give us a certain right to set our hopes as well on a habitable world. With these words I express the congratulations of the Swedish Academy and ask you now to receive this year's Nobel Prize for Literature from the hands of His Royal Highness the Crown Prince.

Heinrich Böll

HEINRICH BÖLL

I was born in December 21, 1917 in Cologne, on the Rhine, the son of the sculptor and cabinet-maker Viktor Böll and his wife Maria, née Hermanns. Between 1924 and 1928 I attended elementary school in Köln Raderthal, and from 1928 to 1937 the state-run Kaiser-Wilhelm classical secondary school in Cologne. In spring 1937 I began as an apprentice bookseller (publishers, retail trade, antiquarian) for the Matth. Lempertz company in Bonn. I left this apprenticeship in spring 1938, started my first attempts to write, gave private lessons, read a great deal. During autumn 1938 I was conscripted into the national labour service, and released in spring 1939 after completing a six-month term of compulsory service. Because the completion of labour service was a precondition for permission to study at the university, I was able to begin my studies of Germanistics and Classical Philology during the summer term of 1939. Late in the summer of 1939 I was conscripted into the German Army shortly before the outbreak of the war. I took part in the Second World War, in autumn 1940 briefly in France, from 1941 to 1942 (after a severe case of typhus) in the replacement units in Germany, from early 1942 until summer 1943 along the English Channel coast in France, between summer 1943 and autumn 1944 in the Soviet Union, Romania and Hungary, from spring 1945 on for a few weeks in western Germany, where I was taken prisoner by the Americans, and interned until October 1945 in a camp in France, and then for a few weeks in October/November 1945 in an English camp in Belgium.

As early as December 1945, I accompanied my wife and a few relatives in their return from evacuation in the countryside to Cologne, where over the years we settled down in a destroyed house. I started to write again, while simultaneously working on repairing the destroyed house, I started my studies again — merely formally, because proof of occupation was necessary to obtain a food rationing card. From 1946 to 1949 I published short stories, and in 1949 my first book, a novella called *Der Zug war pünktlich*. After a first invitation to a meeting of the "Gruppe 47" in 1951, I met many German postwar writers with whom I afterwards became friends. I owe particular thanks, and hereby give them, to Hans Werner Richter, Alfred Andersch and many others that I cannot name in detail. Even if there occurred brief or permanent controversies during or after these meetings, the Gruppe 47 liberated many German authoresses and authors out of their isolation in a destroyed and fragmented postwar Germany. In 1942 I married Annemarie Cech, who has been irreplaceable, not only as my wife and companion, and not only as fellow experiencer and fellow sufferer in the fascist drama during the Nazi reign in Germany, but also for her critical awareness for language.

Our first child, Christoph, died in October 1945. Our sons Raimund, René and Vincent were born in 1947, 1948 and 1950 in the rubble of Cologne and grew up there.

Between 1950 and 1951 I worked as a temporary employee in the Cologne Bureau of Statistics. From summer 1951 on I have lived as a freelance writer with a fixed postal address in Cologne, but with a continually shifting place of work.

Heinrich Böll died in 1985.

AN ESSAY ON THE REASON OF POETRY

Nobel Lecture on 2 May, 1973
by HEINRICH BÖLL, Federal Republic of Germany
Translation

It is said by those who ought to know — and by others, who also ought to know, it is disputed — that in matters which to all appearances are rational, calculable and achieved by the combined efforts of architects, draughtsmen, engineers, workers — accomplishments such as a bridge — there remain a few millimetres or centimetres of incalculability. This incalculability (tiny with regard to the masses being treated and shaped) may stem from the difficulty of calculating with the nicest precision a mass of complicated interlocking chemical and technical details and materials in all their possible reactions, including the effects of the four classical elements (air, water, fire and earth). The problem here seems not merely to be the design, the repeatedly recalculated and checked technical/chemical/statistical composition, but — let me call it this — their incarnation, which can also be called their realisation. This remainder of incalculability, be it only fractions of millimetres, which correspond to unforeseen tiny differences in extension — what shall we call them? What lies hidden in this gap? Is it what we usually call irony, is it poetry, God, resistance, or (to use a popular phrase nowadays) fiction? Someone who ought to know, a painter who had previously been a baker, once told me that even baking breakfast rolls, which is done early in the morning, almost in the night, was extremely dicey business; you had to stick your nose and your backside out into the grey dawn in order more or less instinctively to find the right mixture of ingredients, temperature and baking time, since each and every day demanded its own freshly-baked rolls, an important, even holy element of the first morning meal for all those who shoulder the burden of the new day. Should we also call this almost incalculable element irony, poetry, God, resistance or fiction? How can we cope without it? Not to mention love. No one will ever know how many novels, poems, analyses, confessions, sufferings and joys have been piled up on this continent called Love, without it ever having turned out to be totally investigated.

When I am asked how or why I wrote this or that, I always find myself quite embarassed. I would gladly furnish not merely the questioner, but myself as well, with an exhaustive answer, but can never do so. I cannot recreate the context in its entirety, yet I wish that I could, so that at least the literature I myself make might be made slightly less of a mysterious process than bridge-building and bread-baking.

And because literature in its incarnation as a whole, in its message and shape, can clearly have a liberating effect, it would after all be quite useful to tell people about the genesis of this incarnation, so that more people can share in this process. What is it that I myself, although I demonstrably produce it, cannot even approximately explain? — this something which from the first to the last line I myself set down on paper, vary repeatedly, rework, somewhat shift the emphasis of, yet which as it recedes in time grows alien to me, like something that is gone or past, retreating further and further from me, even as it is perhaps becoming important for others as a shaped message? Theoretically, the total reconstruction of the process would have to be possible, a form of parallel protocol created as the work progresses, and which, if done in detail, would probably be many times larger than the work itself. Not merely the intellectural and mental, but also the sensory and material dimensions would have to be satisfied, mental and physical nourishment and metabolism, the mood and flashes of wit *enlighteningly* provided, the function of one's environment not only in its incarnation as such, but also as backdrop. For example, I often watch sports shows with my mind almost completely blank, in order to practise contemplation with a blank mind, admittedly a rather mystical exercise — yet all these programmes would have to be included in their entirety in the protocol, since after all a kick or a leap might happen to spark some reaction or other in my thoughtless contemplation, or perhaps the movement of a hand, a smile, a commentator's word, a commercial. Every telephone call, the weather, letters, each individual cigarette would have to be included, a passing car, a pneumatic drill, the cackling of a hen that disturbs a context.

The table upon which I am writing this is 76.5 cm high, its top is 69.5 by 111 cm. It has turned legs, a drawer, seems to be seventy to eighty years old, was a possession of a great-aunt of my mother's, who, after her husband had died in a madhouse and she herself had moved into a smaller flat, sold it to her brother, my wife's grandfather. And so, after my wife's grandfather had died, it came into our possession, a despised and rather despicable piece of furniture of no value, knocking around somewhere, no one knows exactly where, until it surfaced during a move and proved to have been damaged by a bomb: somewhere, at some time or other, a piece of shrapnel had bored a hole through its top during the Second World War — already it would seem to be not merely of sentimental value, but an entry into a dimension of political and social history worth relating, using the table as an entrance vehicle, in which connection the deadly contempt of the furniture porters who nearly refused to bring it along would be more important than its present use, which is more of an accident than the stubbornness with which —

and not for reasons of sentiment or memory, but rather for reasons of principle — we kept it from reaching the refuse dump, and as by now I have written a few things on this table, I might be permitted a passing attachment to it, with the emphasis on 'passing'. Not to mention the objects lying on this table; they are incidental and exchangeable, also accidental, with the possible exception of the Remington typewriter, model "Travel Writer de Luxe", produced in 1957, to which I am also attached, this means of production that has long since lost all interest for the tax authorities, although it has played a major part in their acquisition of such income, and still does so. On this instrument that any specialist would regard or touch only with disdain, I have written at a guess four novels and several hundred items, and even so I am attached to it not only for that reason, but again because of principles, as it still works and proves how small the writer's opportunities and ambitions for investment are. I mention the table and the typewriter in order to demonstrate to myself that not even these two necessary utensils are completely understandable to me, and were I to attempt to elucidate their origins with the necessary exact correctness, their precise material, industrial, social process of production and their origins, it would give rise to an almost endless compilation of British and West German industrial and social history. Not to mention the house, the space in which this table stands, the soil on which this house was built, especially not to mention the people who — probably for several centuries — lived in it, the living and the dead, not to mention those who bring the coal, wash the silverware, deliver the letters and newspapers — and especially not to mention those who are close, closer, closest to us. And yet mustn't *everything*, from the table to the pencils, that lie there in their history in its entirety, be brought in, including those close, closer, closest to us? Will there not be enough remainders, gaps, resistances, poetry, God, fiction left — even more than in building bridges and baking rolls?

It's true and it's easily said that language is material, and something does materialise as one writes. Yet how might one explain that — as is occasionally demonstrated — something like life appears, people, fates, actions; that this incarnation occurs on something so deathly pale as paper, where the imagination of the author is linked to that of the reader in a hitherto unexplained manner, a process that cannot be reconstructed in its entirety, where even the wisest, most sensitive interpretation remains only a more or less successful approximation; and how indeed might it be possible to describe, to register the transition from the conscious to the unconscious — in the person writing and the person reading, respectively — with the necessary total exactitude, and furthermore break it down into its national, continental, international, religious or ideological details, not neglecting the continually changing proportions of the two, in these two — the person writing and the person reading — and the sudden reversal where the one becomes the other; and that in this abrupt shift the one is no longer to be distinguished from the other? There will always be a remainder, whether you call it the inexplicable ('secret' would also be fine), there remains and will remain an area, however tiny, into which the reason of our origins will not penetrate, because it runs into the hitherto unexplained reason of peotry and of the art of the imagination, whose incarnation remains as elusive as the body of a woman, a man or even merely of an animal. Writing is — at least for me — movement forward, the conquest of a body that I do not know at all, away from something to something that I do not yet know; I never know what will happen — and here 'happen' is not intended as plot resolution, in the sense of classical dramaturgy, but in the sense of a complicated and complex experiment that with given imaginary, spiritual, intellectual and sensual materials in interaction strives — on paper to boot! — towards incarnation. In this respect there can be no successful literature, nor would there be any successful music or painting, because no one can already have seen the object it is striving to become, and in this respect everything that is superficially called modern, but which is better named living art, is experiment and discovery — and transient, can be estimated and measured only in its historical relativity, and it appears to me irrelevant to speak of eternal values, or to seek them. How will we survive without this gap, this remainder, which can be called irony, be called poetry, be called God, fiction, or resistance?

Countries, too, are always only approaching what they claim to be, and there can be no state which does not leave this gap between the verbal expression of its constitution and its realisation, a space that remains, where poetry and resistance grow — and hopefully flourish. And there exists no form of literature which can succeed without this gap. Even the most precise account do without the atmosphere, without the imagination of the reader, even if the person writing it refuses to use it; and even the most precise account must omit — why, it must omit the exact and detailed description of circumstances that actually are required for the incarnation of the conditions of life... it must compose, transpose elements, and even its interpretation and its working protocol are not communicable, if only because the material called language cannot be reduced to a reliable and generally comprehensible communicative currency: so much history and invented history, national and social history, and historical relativity — which would have to be included — weighs down every word, as I have tried to suggest via the example of my work desk. And determining the range of the message is not only a problem of translation from one language to another, it is a much more weighty problem within languages, where definitions can entail world views, and world views can entail wars — I would merely remind you of the wars after the Reformation, which *although* explicable in terms of power politics and hegemony, *also* are wars about religious definitions. It is therefore, by the way, trivial to claim that after all, we do speak the same language, if we do not also demonstrate the load that each word can bear at the level of regional, and frequently even local history. For me, at least, much of the German I see and hear sounds stranger than Swedish, a language of which I unfortunately understand very little.

Politicians, ideologists, theologians and philosophers try time and again to provide solutions with nothing remaining, prefab solved problems. That is their duty — and it is ours, the writers' — since we know that we are not able to solve anything without remainders or resistance — to penetrate into the gaps. There are too many unexplained and inexplicable remainders, entire provinces of waste. Builders of bridges, bakers of rolls and writers of novels normally finish their jobs, and their remainders are not the most problematic areas. While we struggle over *littérature pure* and *littérature engagée* — one of the false dichotomies to which I shall return in a while — we are still not aware of — or are unawares diverted from — thoughts about *l'argent pur* and *l'argent engagé*. If one really observes and listens to politicians and economists talking about something as supposedly rational as money, then the mystical, or perhaps merely mysterious area within these three occupations already mentioned becomes less and less interesting and astonishingly harmless. Let us take, merely as an example, the amazingly bold recent attack on the dollar (which was modestly called a dollar crisis). Naive layman that I am, something occurred to me that no one called by name: two countries were deeply affected, and most emphatically found it necessary — if we assume that the word 'freedom' is not merely a fiction — to do something so remarkable as to support the dollar, i.e., were asked to open their coffers; and these two countries had something historic in common, namely their defeat in the Second World War, and they are both spoken of as having something else in common: their industriousness and diligence. As for the person it concerns — the one who jingles his pocket money or flashes his tiny bankroll — can't it be made clear to him why, although he is by no means working less for his money, it fetches less bread, milk, coffee, miles in a taxi? How many gaps does the mysticism of money offer, and in which strongrooms is its poetry hidden away? Idealistic parents and educators have always tried to convince us that money is filthy. I have never understood that, because I only received money when I had worked (always excepting the

large sum that I have been awarded by the Swedish Academy), and
for anyone who has no choice other than to work, even the dirtiest
job is clear. They provide a living for the those close to him, and
for him, too. Money is the incarnation of his work, and that is clean.
Between work and what it brings in there admittedly is an unexplained
remainder, which vague formulas such as to earn well or to earn
poorly are far less successful at filling than the gap left by the interpretation of a novel or poem.

Compared to the unexplained gaps of money mysticism, the
unexplained remainders of literature are strikingly harmless, and
even so there are still people who with criminal frivolity let the word
'freedom' roll off their tongue, where submission to a myth and
its claims to power is unequivocally demanded and obtained. They
then call for political insight, precisely when insight and perception
about the problem are blocked. On the bottom line of my cheque
I see four different groups of numbers, 32 characters in all, two
of which resemble hieroglyphs. Five of these thirty-two characters
are meaningful to me: three for my account number, two for the
branch of the bank — what do the other twenty-seven represent,
including quite a few zeroes? I am certain that all of these characters
have a rational, meaningful, or as that lovely phrase would have it,
an enlightening explanation. It's just that in my brain and my consciousness there is no room for this enlightening explanation, and
what remains is the cipher mysticism of a secret science which I
have more trouble penetrating, whose poetry and symbolism remains
more alien to me than Marcel Proust's *Remembrance of Things Past*
or the "Wessobrunn Prayer". What these 32 digits demand of me
is trusting belief in the fact that everything is quite correct, that
there remains no unclarity and, if I only were to make a slight effort,
it all would be clear to me too; and yet for me something mysterious
remains — or perhaps fear, much more fear than any realisation
of poetry could produce in me. However, no successful currency
policy is clear to those whose money is involved.

Thirteen digits on my telephone bill, too, and a few on each of
my various insurance policies, not to mention my tax, car and telephone
numbers — I won't take the trouble to count all these numbers that
I ought to have in my head or at least written down, in order to
be able to note my exact place in society at any time. If we quite
happily multiply these 32 digits and the numbers on my cheque by
six, or let's give a discount and multiply them by four, add in the
numbers of one's birthday, a few contractions for religious
affiliation, civil status — have we then at last grasped the Occident
in the addition and the integration of its reason? Is this reason,
as we perceive and accept it — and it is not only made enlightening
for us, but actually enlightens us — perhaps merely an occidental

arrogance that we have exported to the entire world, via colonialism or missions, or in a mixture of them both as an instrument of subjugation? And for those affected, aren't or wouldn't the differences between Christian, socialist, communist, capitalistic outlooks be small, — and even if the poetry of this reason does at times enlighten them, yet doesn't the reason of their poetry remain the victor? What did the greatest crime of the Indians consist of, when they were confronted with European reason exported to America? They didn't know the value of gold — of money! And they fought against something, against that which we even now are fighting as the most recent product of *our* reason, against the destruction of their world and environment, against the total subjugation of their earth by profit, which was more alien to them than their gods and spirits are to us. And what indeed could have revealed to them the Christian message — the new and joyous tidings — in this insane, hypocritical smugness with which on Sunday people served God, praising him as the Saviour, and on Monday once again opened the banks right on time, the places where they administered the only idea they truly believed in, that of money, possession and profit? For the poetry of water and wind, of buffalo and grass, in which their life found its form, there was only scorn — and now we civilised Westerners in our cities, the end product of our total rationality — for in all fairness it must be said: we have not spared ourselves — we are beginning to sense just how real the poetry of water and wind actually is, and what is incarnated therein. Did, or does, the tragedy of our churches perhaps indeed consist, not of what the Enlightenment might have designated as unreasonable matters, but in the despairing and desperately failed attempt to pursue or even overtake a reason that has never been and never can be merged with something so irrational as the incarnated God? Regulations, law texts, approval of experts, a figure-laden forest of numbered regulations, and the production of prejudices that have been hammered into us and set out along the tracks of history teaching, in order to make people ever more estranged from one another. Even in the extreme western reaches of Europe our rationality is in opposition to another, which we simply label irrational. The horrifying problem of Northern Ireland nevertheless consists of the fact that here two kinds of reason have been entangled and hopelessly attacked one another for centuries.

How many provinces of disparagement and disdain has history bequeathed to us? Continents are hidden under the victorious sign of our rationality. Entire populations remained strangers to one another, supposedly speaking the same language. Where marriage in the Western manner was prescribed as creating order, people ignored the fact that it was a privilege: unattainable, inachievable for those who worked the land, the people called farmhands and

milkmaids, who simply didn't have the money even to buy a pair
of sheets, and if they had saved up or stolen the money, wouldn't
have had the bed to put the sheets on. And so they were left untouched
in their illegitimacy; they produced kids anyway! From above and
from the outside, everything seemed completely settled. Clear answers,
clear questions, clear regulations, catechism as delusion. But please,
no wonders, and poetry only as the sign of the supernatural, never
the natural. And then people are surprised, even long for the old
ways of life, when the disparaged and hidden provinces show signs
of revolt, and then of course either the one party or the other must
gain material and political profit from this revolt. Attempts have
been made to bring order into the still unexplored continent called
sexual love by means of regulations similar to those provided budding
philatelists when they start their first album. Permitted and non-
permitted caresses are defined down to the most meticulous details,
when suddenly, to their mutual horror, theo- and ideology confirm
that on this continent which was regarded as determined, cooled
and ordered, there yet remain a few unextinguished volcanoes —
and volcanoes are simply not to be extinguished with tried and
tested firefighting equipment. And just think of everything passed
off, foisted off on God, this much-abused and pitiable authority:
everything, yes, everything that was a problem: all the guides for
inescapable misery in social, economic or sexual form pointed to
him, everything despicable, contemptible, was palmed off on God,
all the leftover "remainders", and yet at the same time he was being
preached about as the Incarnate, without considering that one cannot
place the burden of man on God, nor the burden of God on man,
if he is to be considered incarnate. And who then can be surprised
if he has survived where godlessness was prescribed and where the
misery of the world and one's own society was put off to an unfulfilled
catechism of equally dogmatic form and a future that was ever further
away, and ever further delayed, until it turned out to be a dismal
present? And once again we can also only be reacting to it with
insufferable arrogance if we here presume to denounce this course
of events as reactionary; and similarly, it is arrogance of the same
kind if the official custodians of God claim as their own this God
who appears to have survived in the Soviet Union, without clearing
away the refuse dump under which he is hidden here, and if they
cite the appearance of God *there* as justification for a societal system
here. Again and again, whether boasting of our convictions as Christians
or atheists, we wish to capitalise on one pigheadedly represented
system of ideas or another. This madness of ours, this arrogance
"in itself" again and again buries both: the incarnate Deity, who
is called God become Man, and the vision set in its place, that of
the future of the entirety of mankind. We who so easily humiliate

others, we are lacking in something: humility — which is not to be confused with subordination or obedience, let alone submission. This is what we have done to the colonised peoples: transformed their humility, the poetry of this humility transformed into their humiliation. We are always eager to subjugate and conquer, hardly a surprise in a civilisation whose first text in a foreign language has long been Julius Caesar's *De Bello Gallico*, and whose first exercise in self-satisfaction — unequivocal and clear answers and questions — was the catechism, one catechism or the other, a primer in infallibility and in complete, pre-fab, pre-explained problems.

I have got a bit away from the building of bridges, baking of rolls and writing of novels, and hinted at gaps, ironies, fictive areas, remnants, divinities, mystifications and resistance of other regions — they appeared to me worse, in greater need of illumination than the slight, unilluminated corners in which not our traditional reason, but the reason of poetry — as in for example a novel — lies hidden. The roughly two hundred figures, group by group (including a few codes), that I ought to have in exact sequences, in my head, or at least on a piece of paper, as a proof of my existence, without exactly knowing what they mean, incorporate little more than a pair of abstract claims and proofs of existence within a bureaucracy that not only claims to be, but actually is reasonable. People refer me to it and teach me to trust it blindly. May I not dare expect that people do not merely trust in, but strengthen the reason of poetry, not by leaving it in peace, but by absorbing a bit of its calmness and the pride of its humbleness, which can only be a humbleness towards those below, and never a humbleness towards those above. Regard for others, politeness and justice reside therein, and the wish to recognise and be recognised.

I do not wish to provide new missionary starting-points and vehicles, but I do believe that in the sense of poetic humbleness, politeness and justice I must say that I see considerable similarity, I see possibilities for rapprochement between the stranger à la Camus, the strangeness of the Kafkaesque official and the incarnated God, who after all remains a stranger and — if one neglects a few outbursts of temper — is polite and literal in a remarkable way. Why else has the Catholic church long — I don't know exactly how long — blocked direct access to the literal nature of the texts they declare holy, or else kept it hidden in Latin and Greek, available only to the initiated? I imagine it is in order to keep out the dangers they sensed in the poetry of the incarnated word, and to protect the reason of their power from the dangerous reason of poetry. And after all it is not accidental that the most important consequence of the Reformation was the discovery of languages and their corporeality. And what empire ever could do without language imperialism, i.e., the diffusion of their own language and suppression of the languages of those ruled? In this — but in no other — connexion I regard the for once not imperialistic, but supposedly anti-imperialistic attempts to denounce poetry, the sensuality of language, its incarnation and the power of the imagination (for language and the power of the imagination are one and the same), and to introduce the false dichotomy of information or poetry, as a new version of "divide et impera". It is the brand-new, but once again almost international arrogance of a New Reason, which may possibly permit the poetry of the Indians as an anti-ruling class force, but withholds its own poetry from the classes to be liberated in its own land. Poetry is not a class privilege, it has never been one. Again and again well-established feudal and bourgeois literatures have renewed themselves out of what they condescendingly called popular language, or, to use more modern phrases, jargon or slang. This process may readily be labeled linguistic exploitation, but nothing about this exploitation is changed by spreading propaganda about the false alternatives: information or poetry/literature. The nostalgia-flavoured disapproval perhaps to be found in the expressions' popular language, slang, jargon does not warrant sending poetry, as well, into the exile of the rubbish heap, nor all the forms and expressions of art. Much about this is papal: withholding incarnation and sensuality from others while developing new catechisms which speak of the only correct and the truly false possibilities of expression. One cannot separate the power of the message from the power of the expression in which the message occurs; this paves the way for something that reminds me of the controversies about the communion in both forms, controversies that are theologically rather boring, but important as examples of rejected incarnations, and which in the Catholic part of the world became reduced to the pallor of the Host, which could not even be called a real piece of bread — not to mention the millions of hectolitres of wind withheld! Therein lay an arrogant misunderstanding, not merely of the substances involved, but even more of that which this substance was intended to incarnate.

No class can be liberated by first withholding something from them, and whether this new school of Manichaeism claims to be a- or anti-religious, it thereby takes over the model of the Church as a ruling class, the model which could end with Hus being burned at the stake and Luther excommunicated. One may readily quarrel about the concept of beauty, develop new aesthetics — they are indeed overdue — but they must not begin by withholding matters, and they must not exclude one thing; the possibility of transferral that literature offers: it transfers us to South or North America, to Sweden, India, Africa. It can *also* transfer us to another class, another time, another religion and another race. It has — even in its bourgeois form — never been its goal to create strangeness, but to remove it. And although one may regard the class from which it is largely derived as overdue for replacement, yet as a product of this class it was in most cases also a hiding-place for resistance to that class. And the internationality of resistance must be preserved, that which keeps or makes one writer — Alexander Solzhenitsyn — a believer, and another — Arrabal — an embittered and bitter enemy of religion and the Church. Nor is this resistance to be comprehended as a mere mechanism or reflex which calls forth belief in God here, lack of belief in God there, but rather as the incarnation of the relationships of intellectual history as they are played out between various rubbish heaps and provinces of rebellion and apostasy... and also as recognition of their interconnections without arrogance and without claims of infallibility. To a political prisoner or perhaps only isolated dissidents in, e.g., the Soviet Union it may seem wrong or even insane when people in the Western world protest against the Vietnam War — psychologically, one can understand his situation in his cell or his social isolation — and yet he would have to realise that the guilt of the one cannot be ticked off against that of the other, and that when people demonstrate for Vietnam, they also demonstrate for him! I know that this sounds utopian, and yet this appears to me to be the only possibility of a new internationality, not neutrality. No author can take over alleged or specious divisions and judgements, and to me it appears almost suicidal that we are even and still discussing the division into committed literature and other kinds. Not only do we, precisely when we think that it is the one, have to intervene for the other with all our might; no, it is precisely through this falsified alternative that we accept a bourgeois principle of divisions, one which turns us into strangers. It is not only the division of our potential strength, but also of our potential — and I'll risk this without even blushing — incarnated beauty, since it too can liberate, just as the communicated thought can: it can be liberating in itself, or as the provocation that it may create. The strength of undivided literature is not the neutralisation of directions, but the internationality of resistance, and to this resistance belong poetry, incarnation, sensuality, imaginative power and beauty. The new Manichaean iconoclasticism which wants to take them away from us, which wants to take all art away from us, would rob not only us, but also those for whom it does what it believes it must do. No curse, no bitterness, not even the information about the desperate situation of a class is possible without poetry, and even to condemn it requires that it first must be recognised. Go and read Rosa Luxemburg carefully and note which statues Lenin ordered erected first: the first for Count Tolstoy, of whom he said that until this count began to write, Russian literature contained no peasants; the second for the "reactionary" Dostoevsky. If one wishes to choose an ascetic road to change, one might personally renounce art and literature, but one cannot do so for others until one has brought them to the knowledge or recognition of what they are to renounce. This renunciation must be voluntary, or else it becomes a papal decree, like a new catechism, and once again an entire continent, such as the continent of Love, would be doomed to a parched sterility. It is not merely for frivolity nor only to shock that art and literature have again and again transformed their *forms*, discovering new ones by experiment. In these forms they have also incarnated something, and that something was almost never the confirmation of what existed and was already available; and if it is extirpated, one gives up a further possibility: artifice. Art is always a good hiding-place, not for dynamite, but for intellectual explosives and social time bombs. Why would there otherwise have been the various Indices? And precisely in their despised and often even despicable beauty and lack of transparency lies the best hiding-place for the barb that brings about the sudden jerk or the sudden recognition.

Before concluding, I must state a necessary limitation. The weakness of my intimations and explanations unavoidably stems from the fact that although I question the tradition of reason in which — hopefully not completely successfully — I was brought up, I am nevertheless using the means of that very same reason, and it would be more than unfair to denounce this reason in all its dimensions. This reason has obviously succeeded in spreading doubt about its all-encompassing claim, about what I have called its arrogance, and in retaining experience in and memory of what I have called the reason of poetry, which I do not regard as a privileged, nor a bourgeois institution. It can be communicated, and precisely because its literalness and incarnation often appear strange, it can prevent or remove strangeness or alienation. After all, *befremdet zu sein* 'being strange' can also involve being astounded, surprised, or merely moved. As for what I have said about humbleness — naturally only by way of suggestion — I say it is not thanks to my religious upbringing or memory, which always meant humiliating when it said humility, but from reading Dostoevsky early and late in life. And it is precisely because I consider as the most important literary shift the international movement for a classless, or no longer class-determined literature, the discovery of entire provinces of humbled people destined to be human waste, that I warn you about the destruction of poetry, about the arid sterility of Manichaeism, about the iconoclasticism of what appears to me to be a blind zeal which won't even tap up the bath water before it throws out the baby. It appears meaningless to me to denounce or to glorify the young or the old. It appears meaningless to me to dream of old ways of life that only can be reconstructed in museums; it appears meaningless to me to create dichotomies such as conservative/progressive. The new wave of nostalgia that clings to furniture, clothes, forms of expression and scales of feeling only serves to demonstrate that the new world grows ever stranger to us. That the reason upon which we have built and relied has not made the world more reliable or familiar; that the rational/irrational dichotomy also was a false one. Here I have had to avoid or abandon a great deal, because one thought always leads to another and we would get carried away if we were to survey every detail of these continents exhaustively. I have had to abandon humour, which also is not the privilege of any class, and yet is ignored in its poetry and as a hiding-place for resistance.

Literature 1973

PATRICK WHITE

"for an epic and psychological narrative art which has introduced a new continent into literature"

THE NOBEL PRIZE FOR LITERATURE

Speech by ARTUR LUNDKVIST, of the Swedish Academy
Translation from the Swedish text

Your Majesty, Your Royal Highnesses, Ladies and Gentlemen,
This year's Nobel Prize for Literature has been awarded by the Swedish Academy to the Australian Patrick White. In the—as always—brief citation, mention is made of "his epic and psychological narrative art which has introduced a new continent into literature". These words have been somewhat misunderstood in certain quarters. They are only intended to emphasize the prominent position occupied by Patrick White in the literature of his country: they should not be taken to deny the existence of an important body of Australian literature apart from his writings.

In fact a long succession of authors have endowed Australian literature with an independence and a character which are unmistakably Australian and by virtue of which that literature has long deserved to be regarded in the eyes of the world as something more than an extension of the English tradition. It will be sufficient here to mention such names as Henry Lawson and Henry Handel Richardson. Lawson was the son of an immigrant Norwegian seaman by the name of Larsen, and in his short stories he gave authentic expression to various types of down-to-earth Australian experience. The authoress writing under the name of Henry Handel Richardson achieved in her most important sequence of novels an authentic and grandiose memorial to her father as the exponent of a lingering British way of life in Australia. Nor should one neglect a number of ambitious but somewhat recondite poets who have heightened Australian awareness and intensified the expressive powers of their language.

For all his originality, there is no denying that the work of Patrick White displays certain typical features of Australian literature generally sharing with it the background, natural history and ways of life of the country. It is also well known that White stands in close relation to advanced Australian pictorial artists such as Sidney Nolan, Arthur Boyd and Russel Drysdale, who with the means at their disposal aim at something of the same expressiveness as he sets out to achieve in his writing. Also it is an encouraging sign that White's influence has gradually made itself felt and that several of the most promising young writers are to be seen as his successors in one way or another.

At the same time, however, it should be emphasized that White is less preoccupied than some of his representative colleagues with things specifically Australian. Although most of his novels are set against an Australian background, his main concern has been to depict people whose problems and living situations are highly individualized, transcending the local and the national. Even in his most typically Australian epic, *The Tree of Man,* in which an important part is played by nature and society, his principal aim has been to portray his characters from the inside, to make them come alive not so much in terms of typical or atypical settler careers as in the guise of unique individuals. And when he accompanies his explorer Voss into the wilderness of the continent, that wilderness becomes first and foremost a dramatic scenario for the obsession and self-sacrifice of a Nietzschean willpower.

One is struck by the frequency with which Patrick White has made his main characters to a greater or lesser degree outsiders in relation to society: aliens, maladjusted or retarded people and quite often mystics and zealots. It is as though in these people, destitute and vulnerable as they are, he found it easiest to discern the human qualities which fascinate him. This is the case with the characters of *Riders in the Chariot,* whose alien status or deviation brings them persecution and suffering but who in a mystical way are also the elect, victorious in their misfortune. It is also the case with the two brothers in *The Solid Mandala,* with their contradictory characters: the well-adjusted but spiritually barren and the clumsy but intuitively percipient. In a way it is also true of the all-pervading principal characters in White's two latest and largest novels: the artist in *The Vivisector* and the old woman in *The Eye of the Storm.* In the artist the creative urge is portrayed as a species of curse, as a result of which his art becomes an all-consuming effort of which both its practitioner and the people close to him become the victims. In the old woman the author has taken the experience of a cyclone as the mystical centre from which an insight radiates to shed light on her life, with its many misadventures, right up to the moment of her death.

Patrick White is a rather difficult author not only because of his special ideas and problems but also perhaps no less due to his unusual combination of epic and poetic qualities. In his broad narrative he uses a highly compressed language, a verbal art worked out to the last detail and constantly aiming for a maximum of expressive effect, a relentless intensification or a subtle penetration. Here beauty and truth are closely allied or completely fused together: a beauty radiating light and life, evoking the poetry inherent in things, in nature and in all manner of phenomena, and truth which exposes and liberates, even though at first it may seem repugnant or frightening.

Patrick White is a social critic mainly through his depiction of human beings, as befits a true novelist. He is first and foremost a bold psychological explorer, at the same time as he readily refers to ideological views of life or mystical convictions to elicit the support and the uplifting message which they have to offer. His relationship to himself, like his relationship to his fellow beings, is complex and full of contradictions. Exalted demands are thrown into sharp relief against emphatic denials. Passion and longing are confronted by a distinct puritanism. In contradistinction to what may be pride in himself he glorifies humility and humiliation, a persistent feeling of guilt that demands atonement and sacrifice. He is constantly assailed by doubts concerning the capacity of thought and art, even though he is indefatigable in his high-minded pursuit of both these things.

Patrick White's literary art has spread his fame throughout the world and he now ranks as Australia's foremost representative in his field. His creative work, performed in solitude and doubtless in the teeth of considerable opposition, in various kinds of adversity, has gradually yielded lasting and progressively more widely acknowledged results, in spite of the doubts he himself may have had concerning the value of his efforts. The controversial side of Patrick White is connected with the extreme tension of his selfexpression, with his assault on the most difficult problems: the very qualities that constitute his indisputable greatness. Without those qualities he would be unable to bestow the consolation now present in the very midst of his gloom: the conviction that there must be something more worth living for than our onward rushing civilization seems to offer.

The Swedish Academy regrets that Patrick White is not here to-day. But as his representative we greet one of his best friends, the excellent Australian artist Sidney Nolan. And now I beg you, Mr. Nolan, to receive the Nobel Prize for Literature, awarded to Patrick White, from the hands of His Majesty the King.

PATRICK WHITE

I was born on May 28th 1912 in Knightsbridge, London, to Australian parents. Victor White was then forty-two, his wife Ruth Withycombe ten years younger. When I was six months old my parents returned to Australia and settled in Sydney, principally because my mother could not face the prospect of too many sisters-in-law on the property in which my father had an interest with three older brothers. Both my father's and my mother's families were yeoman-farmer stock from Somerset, England. My Great-Grandfather White had emigrated to New South Wales in 1826, as a flockmaster, and received a grant of Crown land in the Upper Hunter Valley. None of my ancestors was distinguished enough to be remembered, though there is a pleasing legend that a Withycombe was fool to Edward II. My Withycombe grandfather emigrated later in the Nineteenth Century. After his marriage with an Australian, he and my grandmother sailed for England, but returned when my mother was a year old. Grandfather Withycombe seems to have found difficulty in settling; he drifted from one property to another, finally dying near Muswellbrook on the Upper Hunter. My father and mother were second cousins, though they did not meet till shortly before their marriage. The Withycombes enjoyed less material success than the Whites, which perhaps accounted for my mother's sense of her own superiority in White circles. Almost all the Whites remained wedded to the land, and there was something peculiar, even shocking, about any member of the family who left it. To become any kind of artist would have been unthinkable. Like everybody else I was intended for the land, though vaguely I knew this was not to be.

My childhood was a sickly one. It was found that I was suffering from nothing worse than asthma, but even so, nobody would insure my life. As a result of the asthma I was sent to school in the country, and only visited Sydney for brief, violently asthmatic sojourns on my way to a house we owned in the Blue Mountains. Probably induced by the asthma I started reading and writing early on, my literary efforts from the age of about nine running chiefly to poetry and plays. When thirteen I was uprooted from Australia and put at school at Cheltenham, England, as my mother was of the opinion that what is English is best, and my father, though a chauvinistic Australian, respected most of her caprices. After seeing me 'settled' in my English prison, my parents and sister left for Australia. In spite of holidays when I was free to visit London theatres and explore the countryside, I spent four very miserable years as a colonial at an English school. My parents returned for the long holidays when I was sixteen, and there were travels in Europe, including Scandinavia. Norway and Sweden made a particular impression on me as I had discovered Ibsen and Strindberg in my early teens—a taste my English housemaster deplored: 'You have a morbid kink I mean to stamp out'; and he then proceeded to stamp it deeper in.

When I was rising eighteen I persuaded my parents to let me return to Australia and at least see whether I could adapt myself to life on the land before going up to Cambridge. For two years I worked as jackeroo, first in the mountainous southern New South Wales, which became for me the bleakest place on earth, then on the property of a Withycombe uncle in the flat, blistering north, plagued alternately by drought and flood. I can remenber swimming my horse through flood-waters to fetch the mail, and enjoying a dish of stewed nettles during a dearth of vegetables. The life in itself was not uncongenial, but the talk was endlessly of wool and weather. I developed the habit of writing novels behind a closed door, or at my uncle's, on the dining table. More reprehensible still, after being a colonial at my English school, I was now a 'Pom' in the ears of my fellow countrymen. I hardly dared open my mouth, and welcomed the opportunity of escaping to King's College, Cambridge. Even if a university should turn out to be another version of a school, I had decided I could lose myself afterwards as an anonymous particle of the London I already loved.

In fact I enjoyed every minute of my life at King's, especially the discovery of French and German literature. Each vacation I visited either France or Germany to improve my languages. I wrote fitfully, bad plays, worse poetry. Then, after taking my degree, the decision had to be made: what to do? It was embarrassing to announce that I meant to stay in London and become a writer when I had next to nothing to show. To my surprise my bewildered father, who read little beyond newspapers and stud-books, and to whom I could never say a word if we found ourselves stranded alone in a room, agreed to let me have a small allowance on which to live while trying to write.

At this period of my life I was in love with the theatre and was in and out of it three or four nights of the week. I tried unsuccessfully to get work behind the scenes. I continued writing the bad plays which fortunately nobody would produce, just as no one did me the unkindness of publishing my early novels. A few sketches and lyrics appeared in topical revues, a few poems were printed in literary magazines. Then, early in 1939, a novel I had managed to finish, called *Happy Valley*, was published in London, due to the fact that Geoffrey Grigson the poet, then editor of the magazine *New Verse* which had accepted one of my poems, was also reader for a publishing firm. This novel, although derivative and in many ways inconsiderably, was received well enough by the critics to make me feel I had become a writer. I left for New York expecting to repeat my success, only to be turned down by almost every publisher in that city, till the Viking Press, my American publishers of a lifetime, thought of taking me on.

This exhilarating personal situation was somewhat spoilt by the outbreak of war. During the early, comparatively uneventful months I hovered between London and New York writing too hurriedly a second novel *The Living and the Dead.* In 1940 I was commissioned as an air force intelligence officer in spite of complete ignorance of what I was supposed to do. After a few hair-raising weeks amongst the RAF great at Fighter Command I was sent zig-zagging from Greenland to the Azores in a Liverpool cargo boat with a gaggle of equally raw intelligence officers, till finally we landed on the Gold Coast, to be flown by exotic stages to Cairo, in an aeroplane out of Jules Verne.

The part I played in the War was a pretty insignificant one. My work as an operational intelligence officer was at most useful. Much of the time was spent advancing or retreating across deserts, sitting waiting in dust-ridden tents, or again in that other desert, a headquarters. At least I saw something of almost every country in the Middle East. Occasionally during those years bombs or gunfire created what should have been a reality, but which in fact made reality seem more remote. I was unable to write, and this finally became the explanation of my state of mind: my flawed self has only ever felt intensely alive in the fictions I create.

Perhaps the most important moments of my war were when, in the Western Desert of Egypt, I conceived the idea of one day writing a novel about a megalomaniac German, probably an explorer in Nineteenth Century Australia, and when I met my Greek friend Manoly Lascaris who has remained the mainstay of my life and work.

After demobilisation we decided to come to Australia where we bought a farm at Castle Hill outside Sydney. During the war I had thought with longing of the Australian landscape. This, and the grave-yard of post-war London, and the ignoble desire to fill my belly, drove me to burn my European bridges. In the meantime, in London, in Alexandria on the way out, and on the decks of liners, I was writing *The Aunt's Story*. It was exhilarating to be free to express myself again, but nobody engaged in sorting themselves out of the rubble left by a world war could take much interest in novels. Australians, who were less involved, were also less concerned. Most of them found the book unreadable, just as our speech was unintelligible during those first years at Castle Hill. I had never felt such a foreigner. The failure of *The Aunt's Story* and the need to learn a language afresh made me wonder whether I should ever write another word. Our efforts at farming—growing fruit, vegetables, flowers, breeding dogs and goats, were amateurish, but consuming. The hollow in which we lived, or perhaps the pollen from the paspalum which was always threatening to engulf us, or the suspicion that my life had taken a wrong turning, encouraged the worst attacks of asthma I had so far experienced. In the eighteen years we spent at Castle Hill, enslaved more than anything by the trees we had planted, I was in and out of hospitals. Then about 1951 I began writing again, painfully, a novel I called in the beginning *A Life Sentence on Earth*, but which developed into *The Tree of Man*. Well received in England and the United States, it was greeted with cries of scorn and incredulity in Australia: that somebody, at best a dubious Australian, should flout the naturalistic tradition, or worse, that a member of the grazier class should aspire to a calling which was the prerogative of schoolteachers! *Voss*, which followed, fared no better: it was 'mystical, ambiguous, obscure'; a newspaper printed its review under the headline 'Australia's most Unreadable Novelist'. In *Riders in the Chariot* it was the scene in which Himmelfarb the Jewish refugee is subjected to a mock crucifixion by drunken workmates which outraged the blokes and the bluestockings alike. Naturally, 'it couldn't happen here'—except that it does, in all quarters, in many infinitely humiliating ways, as I, a foreigner in my own country, learned from personal experience.

A number of Australians, however, discovered they were able to read a reprint of *The Aunt's Story*, a book which had baffled them when first published after the War, and by the time *The Solid Mandala* appeared, it was realised I might be something they had to put up with.

In 1964, submerged by the suburbs reaching farther into the country, we left Castle Hill, and moved into the centre of the city. Looking back, I must also have had an unconscious desire to bring my life full circle by returning to the scenes of my childhood, as well as the conscious wish to extend my range by writing about more sophisticated Australians, as I have done in *The Vivisector* and *The Eye of the Storm*. On the edge of Centennial Park, an idyllic landscape surrounded by a metropolis, I have had the best of both worlds. I have tried to celebrate the park, which means so much to so many of us, in *The Eye of the Storm* and in some of the shorter novels of *The Cockatoos*. Here I hope to continue living, and while I still have the strength, to people the Australian emptiness in the only way I am able.

Patrick White died in 1990.

Literature 1974

EYVIND JOHNSON

"for a narrative art, far-seeing in lands and ages, in the service of freedom"

HARRY MARTINSON

"for writings that catch the dewdrop and reflect the cosmos"

THE NOBEL PRIZE FOR LITERATURE

Speech by KARL RAGNAR GIEROW, of the Swedish Academy
Translation from the Swedish text

Your Majesty, Your Royal Highnesses, Ladies and Gentlemen,
Eyvind Johnson's education — that is, the education provided by society at
that time — ended when he was thirteen and was imparted to him at a little
village school north of the Arctic Circle. The future awaiting the young Harry
Martinson opened up to him when, at the age of six, as a so-called child of
the parish, he was sold by auction to the lowest bidder — that is, to the person
who took charge of the forsaken boy for the smallest payment out of parochial
funds. The fact that, with such a start in life, both of them have their places
on this platform today, is the visible testimony to a transformation of society,
which, step by step, is still going on all over the world. With us it came unusually
early; it is perhaps our country's biggest blessing, perhaps also its most remarkable
achievement during the last thousand years.

Eyvind Johnson and Harry Martinson did not come alone, nor first. They
are representative of the many proletarian writers or working-class poets who,
on a wide front, broke into our literature, not to ravage and plunder, but to
enrich it with their fortunes. Their arrival meant an influx of experience and
creative energy, the value of which can hardly be exaggerated. To that extent
they are representative also of the similar breakthrough that has later occurred
in the whole of our cultural world. A new class has conquered Parnassus. But
if by a conqueror we mean the one who gained most from the outcome, then
Parnassus has conquered a new class.

To determine an author and his work against the background of his social
origin and political environment is at present good form. And what is good
form is seldom particularly to the point. "Eyvind Johnson's literary achievement is one of the most significant and characteristic of a very fruitful period
in the whole of Europe." This last sentence is not mine; it was written thirty
years ago by Lucien Maury. Even then the boy from a primary school in a
remote village in the far north of Sweden was an experienced and self-
assured European, never forgetful of his origin (of which his autobiographical
stories provide a lasting document), but still less bound and inhibited by the
environment where he took his first steps. International perspective distinguished Eyvind Johnson's further writings, and it is matched by an equally
wide outlook in time, over the destinies and ages of the human race. The
renewal of the historical novel, which he has carried out on his own and
perhaps exemplified most clearly in great works like *Days of His Grace* and
Steps Towards Silence, is based not only on extensive research but also on a
clear-sightedness which, expressed briefly, sets out to show that everything
that happens to us has happened before, and everything that took place once

in the world is still taking place, recognizable under changed signs, a constant simultaneity of epochs which may be the only wisdom the past can teach us in our attempts to survey the present and divine an era which we have not yet seen.

If, nevertheless, we are to point to a special phase and one particular mental environment whose traces are ineffaceable in Eyvind Johnson's work with his pen, it is that very period when Lucien Maury discovered that in this Nordic writer Europe had one of its important intellectuals. The French time-analyst described this epoch as very fruitful. What was it that made it so productive? Not favourable conditions, but the indomitable resistance to the conditions that prevailed. D-day had not yet dawned; nazism still had a stranglehold on Europe. It was in that predicament that Eyvind Johnson spoke out. His attitude was so passionate that its fervour has never since vanished from what he wrote. He retained his European perspective, but naturally it was Scandinavia's liberty that was dearest to him just then. He endorsed his conviction with a handshake across the border. Together with a co-editor on the Norwegian side he was responsible during the occupation years for a mouthpiece of the new Scandinavianism, called—"A Handshake". As from today the two publishers of that little paper are both Nobel prize-winners. The name of Eyvind Johnson's co-editor on the Norwegian side of the frontier was Willy Brandt.

Both Eyvind Johnson and still more Harry Martinson have a lot in common with the oldest and perhaps greatest of all proletarian writers, the subtly wise and charming author of ingenious fables, Aesop. Like him, they spin webs, capturing you with beguiling words that always contain other and more than what they literally say. But the differences between this year's two literary prizewinners are greater than the similarities. Beside Eyvind Johnson, whose writing is based so very much on his fiercely defended citizenship in a free society, Harry Martinson may appear to be almost a purely asocial individual, the incorrigible vagrant in our literature. No one has succeeded in putting him under lock and key. The philosophic tramp Bolle in *The Road* is in many ways the author's spokesman, and he is not homeless at the gate. He is home-less only when he gets inside four walls. He is the bearer of asocialism as a wish and a principle that brings good luck; he is a vagabond of his own free will, in agreement with life's sound instincts and in spontaneous revolt against what is trying to stifle them—that which is governed by calculation and established by force. He already has his home; it is beyond and outside, and he is always on the way towards it. From this starting point, though in a different key, we can also conceive the tragically beautiful vision of Aniara, of the spaceship which heads away from an increasingly hostile existence on a frozen earth and itself loses its rudder, cut off from its home port and with its destination lost.

"I don't want to have real that most people want to have real", Bolle re-marks. In saying this he has also said quite a lot about Harry Martinson's writing. Realism is to be found there to the extent that it can be called elemental: it is based on the closest familiarity with the four elements.

Harry Martinson got to know earth and air as a tramp on the roads, fire and water as a stoker at sea. Yet the world of imagination is more important and more real to him than that of reality. Where realism plods methodically along, his imagination races with the swallow-winged glide of the skater. However, it is not a flight from truth; on the contrary. "We must learn the essential difference between what is factual and what is truth", he has said. "We have facts everywhere. They whirl in our eyes like sand." But it is truth we are concerned with, and that is something else, it is a state in nature and in the receptive human being; it is

> the good will with presence and peace of mind
> to keep watch and to be.

For Harry Martinson fact and fiction are one, and without any aphoristic hair-splitting an entire outlook on life is summed up in these pregnant words. The last two, most emphasized, form the simple verb of mere existence: to be. But existence is only fit for human beings if it gives them pleasure, and for that, good will and vigilance are needed. So, in the end, the truth to which this wanderer's path has led him is a gratitude, round-eyed as a child's, for the generous life that has constantly given him trials, riddles and joy in good measure.

After this quickly cut-out silhouette of two remarkable literary profiles, it is my very pleasant duty to express the heartfelt congratulations of the Swedish Academy to Eyvind Johnson and Harry Martinson and to ask them to receive the emblems of the 1974 Nobel Prize for Literature from the hands of His Majesty the King.

EYVIND JOHNSON

Translation

Born in 1900 at Svartbjörsbyn near Boden in the north of Sweden.

Parents: Olof Petter J., stonecutter from Värmland, and Cevia Gustafsdotter from Blekinge. Six children, of whom E. J. was the youngest but one. His father fell ill with silicosis about 1904 and E. J. was taken care of by his childless aunt and her husband, stonecutter Anders Johan Rost. At the age of fourteen he left his foster-parents, of whom he was very fond, to look for work near the home where he was born.

He did many different kinds of work, first at the timber sorting boom near Sävast on the Lule River, then at the Björn brickworks. Between 1915 and 1919 he was a sawmill worker, a ticket seller and usher at a cinema, and a projectionist, then he was assistant to plumbers and electricians. In 1918 he was a locomotive cleaner at the engine sheds in Boden, and for a time during the winter, a stoker on goods trains between Boden and Haparanda. Again sawmill worker for a while, then hay-presser, then out of work. Borrowing money, he travelled down to Stockholm, where he got work at LM Ericsson's big workshop in Tulegatan. The metalworkers' strike broke out in 1920 and he tried to live on what he wrote, with very meagre results. At the same time, together with some other young budding writers, he founded the literary magazine *Vår Nutid* (Our Present Day), which appeared for six numbers. He then belonged to the society of future writers which called itself *De gröna* (The Green Ones).

From the autumn of 1920 to the autumn of 1921, together with two or three friends, he worked at hay-making and timber-felling on a small farm in Uppland, where he had spare time and peace in which to read and write.

In the autumn of 1921 he went to Germany—cargo boat to Kiel, train to Berlin, and a few months later he continued via the Rhineland to Paris, where he earned his living writing for Swedish papers, as a cement worker and then as a dish-washer at a big hotel near the Gare du Nord. Then back to Berlin, where he remained until the autumn of 1923, when he returned home to Sweden.

His first book *De fyra främlingarna* (The Four Strangers), a collection of short stories, was finished in the spring of 1924 and published during the autumn. During a winter visit to the North, he finished his second book, which was published in the autumn of 1925. By then E. J. was back in France, where he was to live for over five years.

In 1927 he was married at Saint-Leu-La Forêt to Aase Christofersen. Their son Tore was born there in 1928.

In 1930 the family moved home to Sweden.

After Aase Johnson's death E. J. married Cilla Frankenhaeuser. They have two children, Maria, born 1944, and Anders, born 1946.

From 1947 to 1950 E. J. and his family lived in Switzerland and England, and after that at Saltsjöbaden.

Eyvind Johnson died in 1976.

Bibliography

De fyra främlingarna (The Four Strangers), 1924
Timans och rättfärdigheten (Timans and Righteousness), 1925
Stad i mörker (Town in Darkness), 1927
Stad i ljus (Town in Light), 1928; French translation: *Lettre recommandée*, 1927
Minnas (Remembering), 1928
Kommentar till ett stjärnfall (Commentary on a Falling Star), 1929
Avsked till Hamlet (Farewell to Hamlet), 1930
Natten är här (Night is here), 1932
Bobinack, 1932
Regn i gryningen (Rain at Dawn), 1933
Romanen om Olof (The Novel of Olof): 1. *Nu var det 1914* (The Year was 1914),
    1934; 2. *Här har du ditt liv!* (Here is Your Life!), 1935; 3. *Se dig inte om!* (Don't
    Look Back!), 1936; 4. *Slutspel i ungdomen* (Postlude to Youth), 1937
Nattövning (Night Manœuvre), 1938
Den trygga världen (The Safe World), 1940
Soldatens återkomst (The Return of the Soldier), 1940
Krilonromanen (The Novel of Krilon): 1. *Grupp Krilon* (Group Krilon), 1941;
    2. *Krilons resa* (Krilon's Journey), 1942; 3. *Krilon själv* (Krilon Himself), 1943
Strändernas svall (English translation: *Return to Ithaca*): novel, 1946; stage
    version, 1948
Dagbok från Schweiz (Swiss Diary), 1949
Drömmar om rosor och eld (Dreams of Roses and Fire), 1949
Lägg undan solen (Put Away the Sun), 1951
Romantisk berättelse (A Romantic Story), 1953
Tidens gång (The Course of Time), 1955
Vinterresa i Norrbotten (A Winter Journey in Norrbotten), 1955
Molnen över Metapontion (The Clouds Over Metapontion), 1957
Vägar över Metaponto – en resedagbok (Roads by Metaponto – A Travel Diary), 1959
Hans Nådes tid (English translation: *The Days of His Grace*), 1960
Spår förbi Kolonos – en berättelse (Traces Past Colonus – A Story), 1961
Livsdagen lång (Life's Long Day), 1964
Stunder, vågor – anteckningar, berättelser (Moments, Waves – Notes, Stories), 1965
Favel ensam (Favel Alone), 1968
Resa hösten 1921 (Journey in the Autumn of 1921), 1973
Några steg mot tystnaden (Some Steps Towards Silence), 1973

Harry Martinson

HARRY MARTINSON
Translation

Harry Martinson was born at Jämshög in 1904. He was left an orphan at an early age, and after a chequered childhood, in which the children's homes and institutions were as numerous as the escapes, he went to sea at the age of sixteen, spending six years of his life on board various ships and as a workman in foreign countries.

It was from these travels and years of work in environments of all kinds that he later drew material and inspiration for his literary efforts — a couple of books of prose with glimpses, views and memories of the world of coal-heated ships during the 1920s.

These accounts were followed a few years later by one or two books with an autobiographical strain and fictional recollections of a boarded-out child's existence, especially the child's own way of perceiving and trying to understand life and the people in it.

Side by side with this psychological cognition of the childhood land of memory, there appeared some collections of poetry which were continued by degrees in a series of nature studies in prose, in which words and observation are combined in what the author has called "thinking out in the meadow".

In a later work, the novel *Vägen till Klockrike*, the description of the human side is devoted entirely to the relationship between the settled and the itinerant man within ourselves.

A world of journeying in a still wider sense emerges in *Aniara*, an epic work about an imagined space flight with a perspective in depth towards our own time. In it, jostling for room in our consciousness, are our fears and our questions as to where we are heading, together with the planet that our generation is treating as it does.

Harry Martinson died in 1978.

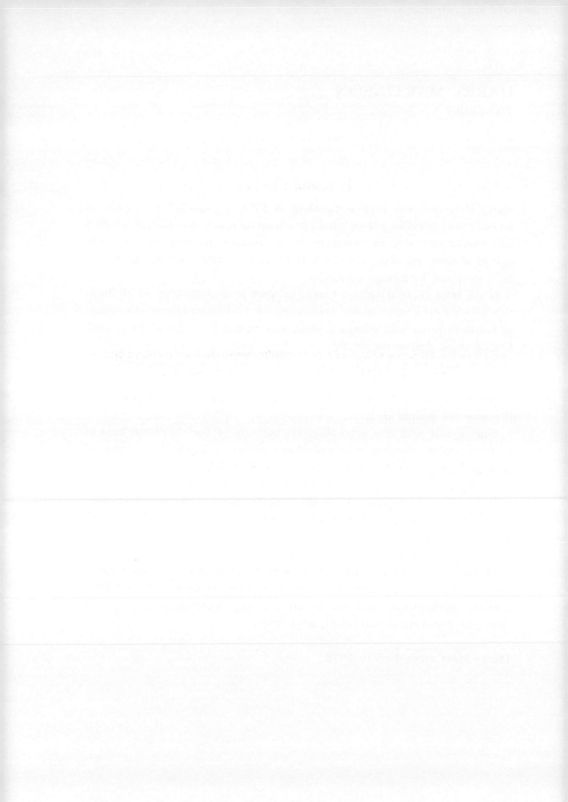

Literature 1975

EUGENIO MONTALE

"for his distinctive poetry which, with great artistic sensitivity, has interpreted human values under the sign of an outlook on life with no illusions"

THE NOBEL PRIZE FOR LITERATURE

Speech by ANDERS ÖSTERLING, of the Swedish Academy
Translation from the Swedish text

Your Majesties, Your Royal Highnesses, Ladies and Gentlemen,
As we all know, this year's Nobel Prize for Literature has been awarded to Eugenio Montale, from Italy. He comes from Eastern Liguria, a coastal landscape whose harsh character is reflected in his poetry. In this there echoes through the years a musical surge of waves which confronts his own destiny with the stern and beauteous majesty of the Mediterranean. Montale's famous first book from 1925 bears too the strange title *Ossi di seppia,* which means "Bones of the Cuttlefish" and clearly emphasizes his distinctive Ligurian character.

At the outset of his career he encountered the fascist dictatorship's atmosphere of suppression of free speech and enforced standardization. Montale refused to write to order and therefore came to belong to the picked troop of free authors who, in spite of everything, managed to hold their own under cover of the so-called hermeticism. His personality was hardened by bitter experience. He served in the first world war as an infantry officer in the Tyrolean Alps, and later became head of the famous Vieusseux Library in Florence. In 1939 he was abruptly dismissed; not having a fascist party membership card he could not be regarded as an Italian citizen. Not until 1948 was he appointed an editor of *Corriere della sera,* the big Milan newspaper, in which for many years he has made a name for himself as an outstanding writer on cultural matters and as a music critic.

Montale has slowly confirmed his key position in Italy's modern literature during this epoch, in many ways so tragic for his native land. To a great extent he can be said to represent this sombre awareness, which seeks individual expression of collective sorrows and troubles. As a poet he interprets this awareness with calm dignity and without any political publicity. He has also gained a seriously listening audience, a fact remarkable in that his lyrical writing is restricted to five books of poems at long intervals. The foremost work is undoubtedly *La bufera e altro* ("The Storm and Other Things"), which was published in 1956. Nor does his reserved and thoughtful temperament court popularity.

Montale himself once stated that as an Italian he wanted before anything else to "wring the neck of eloquence in the old rhetorical language, even at the risk of finding himself in an anti-eloquence". Actually he has gladly taken that risk, and his latest book of poems, *Diario,* a diary from the years 1971 to 1972 consists largely of ironic remarks and epigrams in which the ageing poet lets himself go and criticizes contemporary reality with an almost anti-poetic tendency. His winged horse is a fairly restless spirit, which refuses to stand still docilely in the stall of honour.

But at his best Montale, with strict discipline, has attained a refined artistry, at once personal and objective, in which every word fills its place as precisely as the glass cube in a coloured mosaic. The linguistic laconicism cannot be carried any further; every trace of embellishment and jingle has been cleared away. When, for instance, in the remarkable portrait-poem of the Jewes Dora Markus, he wants to indicate the current background of time, he does so in five words: *Distilla veleno una fede feroce* ("A fierce faith distils poison"). In such masterpieces both the fateful perspective and the ingeniously concentrated structure are reminiscent of T. S. Eliot and "The Waste Land", but Montale is unlikely to have received impulses from this quarter and his development has, if anything, followed a parallel path.

During the half-century in which he has worked, Montale's attitude can be summed up as a fundamental pessimism on the classical line from Leopardi. This pessimism is seldom purely emotional, but manifests itself as a deeply mature, rational insight retaining the critical right both to ask and defy. His conviction is that poor humanity is slipping downhill, that the lessons of history have little value, and that world destitution is going from bad to worse. When he surveys the present juncture he finds that the real evil lies in the fact that the scale of values of another age can be completely lost; in other words, the memory of the great spirits of the past in their striving to build up something which enables us to create another picture of our earthly existence and its conditions.

But his resignation does contain a spark of confidence in life's instinct to go on, to overcome the accumulated obstacles. Montale would not be the born poet he is, if he did not believe deep down that poetry—without being a mass medium—even in our time is still a gentle power which, unperceived, can act as one of the voices of human conscience, faintly heard admittedly, but indestructible and indispensable.

Dear Mr Montale! In the all too brief time at my disposal I have tried to present your poetry and to justify our award. It only remains for me now to express the heartfelt congratulations of the Swedish Academy and to ask you to receive this year's Nobel Prize for Literature from the hands of His Majesty the King.

Eugenio Montale

EUGENIO MONTALE

Eugenio Montale, born in 1896, is one of the few obvious "true masters" of the last fifty years of Italian literature. Born in Genoa into a family of businessmen, he discontinued his secondary studies and started, on a private basis, to study singing with the baritone Ernesto Sivori. But the 1915—18 war (in which he served as an infantry officer), the death of Sivori and his decision to go in for a literary career turned Montale away from that course, in which he had shown an extraordinary interest in melodrama, even its technical aspects. When he started to devote himself to poetry, he was already in possession of a rich and versatile culture and a taste for Bellini's and Debussy's music, impressionist painting and the art of the great novelists of nineteenth-century Europe, at the same time sharing the interests of the Ligurian poets Roccatagliata-Cecardi, Boine and Sbarbaro. However, the "regional" outlook of the poetry of his time was not allowed to limit the critical attention that he paid to Leopardi and Foscolo. It was not until after the war that the poet dedicated himself fully to creative activities and literature. In 1921, he contributed to "Primo Tempo", with Solmi and Debenedetti, revealing, besides his poetic gifts, a rare critical talent through his acuteness and independence of conventional patterns. His *Omaggio a Svevo*, published in 1925 in the Milanese paper "L'Esame", aroused much attention, determining, among other things, the fortune of the works of the Triestine writer.

Montale settled down in Florence in 1928, where he became director of the Gabinetto Vieusseux library. He was one of the first inspirers of "Solaria", always being one of the most active and politically nonconformist Florentine intellectuals until, in 1938, refusing to join the party then in power, he was dismissed from his directorship at the Gabinetto Vieusseux.

In 1925, he published his first collection of poems, *Ossi di seppia*, and quickly became one of the "classics" of contemporary Italian poetry; in his verses, sentiment appears desiccated by a severe intellectual rigour, evoked with intimate fullness in the fervid and striking sights of the Mediterranean landscape. Some critics aptly saw in *Ossi di seppia* a singular introspective continuity, as in a great modern novel, linked to the story of the protagonist, finding its most developed form in the poem "Arsenio".

When *Le occasioni* (1939) was published, it brought consistent confirmation of this inner line of development which, bearing a new classical-modern imprint, identified itself with the great contemporary metaphysical poetry. In *Le occasioni*, Italian poetry and culture as a whole were, from then on, to recognise a book that reflected the solitude and the agony over the human condition of one who lucidly opposed Fascist oppression, creating a song of noble stoicism.

Montale's biography is a chronicle of poetry. The Second World War saw the publication, in 1943, of *Finisterre*, a collection which, published in Lugano in two successive editions of modest print runs, constituted one of the cornerstones of the volume *La bufera e altro*, a consistent continuation of his whole work, printed in 1956. *La farfalla di Dinard* — which from the ninety-six pages of the 1956 edition was expanded, from one edition to another, into the 273 pages of the 1960 edition — showed Montale to be an original writer of autobiography and imaginative prose, almost a narrator, with malicious flashes of wit but with an elegiac spirit.

In 1961, Montale was awarded an honorary degree at the University of Rome and shortly afterwards, at the universities of Milan, Cambridge, and Basel. In 1967, President Saragat appointed him senator for life "in recognition of his distinguished achievements in the literary and artistic fields". This event relieved him, in a sense, of the obligation to go every day to the editorial office of the "Corriere della Sera", where he had been working as a music critic, editor and special correspondent since 1948. The following works, prose as well as poetry, confirmed the vitality of a writer who, true to the fundamental themes of his early career (the Universe marked by inevitable failure and pain as an existential stigma), managed to collect experiences and important moments from the spiritual transformations of our times. *Auto da fé* (1966 and 1972), *Fuori di casa* (1969 and 1975) and *Quaderno di traduzioni* (1948 and 1975) are books that give an idea of the vastness of his interests and of the versatility of his talent, later confirmed by *La bufera e altro* (1970).

In 1971, Mondadori published his fourth collection of poetry, *Satura*, which soon became a bestseller. The book, exhibiting the usual linguistic ambiguity typical of Montale, alludes to a poetry that disrupts its own and others' patterns, including, in a paradoxical manner, much more than is usual (even for Montale) to include in the stylistic and linguistic models of poetry: meditative solicitations, existential themes about man still in some way Christian and Western, a wisdom anything but senile, subtle and provocative humor in the face of a world that changes and proceeds along its tragic and mysterious route.

Montale's great poetry, in actual fact, is born out of the search for those presences that reveal and liberate the hidden world, such as spectres and amulets. Not insusceptible to the stylistic lessons of Pascoli and Gozzano, nor to contemporaries writing in English, Montale has in his turn influenced younger Italian poets, even post-*Ermetismo* poets and experimentators.

After a volume of cultural articles, *La farfalla di Dinard*, he published in 1973, still with Mondadori, *Diario 1971—72*, which contains more recent lyric poems, born of a moral meditation not very different from that which brought forth the poems of *Satura*.

Attentive to the effects of history, Montale's poetry stands out as congenial to spirits that are aware of the consequences (of which, from many aspects, we have not yet seen the end) of the second world tragedy, which the writer saw as temporary reflections of an evil without origin and without end, according to a parable which makes him belong to the more conscious part of the European intellect.

Further works:

Quaderno di quattro anni/ It Depends. A Poet's Notebook, tr. (poetry), 1977; *L'opera in versi/ Collected Poems* (poetry), 1980

Eugenio Montale died in 1981.

IS POETRY STILL POSSIBLE?

Nobel Lecture, December 12, 1975
by
EUGENIO MONTALE
Italy

The Nobel Prize has been awarded this year for the seventy-fifth time, if I am not misinformed. And if there are many scientists and writers who have earned this prestigious recognition, the number of those who are living and still working is much smaller. Some of them are present here and I extend my greetings and best wishes to them. According to widespread opinion, the work of soothsayers who are not always reliable, this year or in the years which can be considered imminent, the entire world (or at least that part of the world which can be said to be civilized) will experience a historical turning of colossal proportions. It is obviously not a question of an eschatological turning, of the end of man himself, but of the advent of a new social harmony of which there are presentiments only in the vast domains of Utopia. At the date of the event the Nobel Prize will be one hundred years old and only then will it be possible to make a complete balance sheet of what the Nobel Foundation and the connected prize have contributed to the formation of a new system of community life, be it that of universal well-being or malaise, but of such an extent as to put an end, at least for many centuries, to the centuries-long diatribe on the meaning of life. I refer to human life and not to the appearance of the amino-acids which dates back several thousand million years, substances which made possible the apparition of man and perhaps already contained the project of him. In this case how long the step of the *deus absconditus* is! But I do not intend to stray from my subject and I wonder if the conviction on which the statute of the Nobel Prize is based is justified: and that is that sciences, not all on the same level, and literary works have contributed to the spread and defence of new values in a broad "humanistic" sense. The response is certainly affirmative. The register of the names of those who, having given something to humanity, have received the coveted recognition of the Nobel Prize would be long. But infinitely more numerous and practically impossible to identify would be the legion, the army of those who work for humanity in infinite ways even without realizing it and who never aspire to any possible prize because they have not written works, acts or academic treatises and have never thought of "making the presses groan", as the Italian expression says. There certainly exists an army of pure, immaculate souls, and they are an obstacle (certainly insufficient) to the spread of that utilitarian spirit which in various degrees is pushed to the point of corruption, crime and every form of violence and intolerance. The academicians of Stockholm have often said no to intolerance, cruel fanaticism and that persecuting spirit which turns the strong against the weak, oppressors against the oppressed. This is true particularly in their choice of literary works, works which can sometimes be murderous, but never like that atomic bomb which is the most mature fruit of the eternal tree of evil.

I will not insist on this point because I am neither a philosopher, sociologist nor moralist.

I have written poems and for this I have been awarded a prize. But I have also been a librarian, translator, literary and musical critic and even unemployed because of recognized insufficiency of loyalty to a regime which I could not love. A few days ago a foreign journalist came to visit me and she asked me, "How did you distribute so many different activities? So many hours for poetry, so many hours for translation, so many for clerical activity and so many for life?" I tried to explain to her that it is to plan a life-time as one plans an industrial project. In the world there is a large space for the useless, and indeed one of the dangers of our time is that mechandizing of the useless to which the very young are particularly sensitive.

At any rate I am here because I have written poems. A completely useless product, but hardly ever harmful and this is one of its characteristics of nobility. But it is not the only one, since poetry is a creation or a sickness which is absolutely endemic and incurable.

I am here because I have written poems: six volumes, in addition to innumerable translations and critical essays. They have said that it is a small production, perhaps supposing that the poet is a producer of merchandise; the machines must be utilized to the full extent. Fortunately, poetry is not merchandise. It is a phenomenon of which we know very little, so much so that two philosophers as different as Croce, a historicist and idealist, and Gilson, a Catholic, are in agreement in considering it impossible to write a history of poetry. For my part, if I consider poetry as an object, I maintain that it is born of the necessity of adding a vocal sound (speech) to the hammering of the first tribal music. Only much later could speech and music be written in some way and differentiated. Written poetry appears, but the relationship in common with music makes itself felt. Poetry tends to open in architectonic forms, there arise the meters, the strophes, the so-called fixed forms. Already in the *Nibelungenlied* and then in Romance epic cycles, the true material of poetry is sound. But a poem which also addresses itself to the eye will not be long in appearing with the Provençal poets. Slowly poetry becomes visual because it paints images, but it is also musical: it unites two arts into one. Naturally the formal structures made up a large part of poetic visibility. After the invention of printing, poetry becomes vertical, does not fill the white space completely, it is rich in new paragraphs and repetitions. Even certain empty spaces have a value. Prose, which occupies all the space and does not give indications of its pronounceability, is very different. And at this point the metrical structures can be an ideal instrument for the art of narration, that is for the novel. This is the case for that narrative instrument which is the eight-line stanza, a form which was already a fossil in the early Nineteenth Century in spite of the success of Byron's *Don Juan* (a poem which remained half-finished).

But towards the end of the Nineteenth Century, the fixed forms of poetry no longer satisfied the eye or the ear. An analogous observation can be made for English blank verse and for the corresponding verse form, *endecasillabo sciolto*. And in the meantime painting was making great strides towards the dissolution of naturalism, and the repercussion was immediate in pictorial art. Thus with a long process, which would require too much time to describe here, one arrived at the conclusion that it was impossible to reproduce reality, real objects, thus creating useless duplicates: but there are displayed *in vitro* or even life-size the objects or figures of which Caravaggio or Rembrandt would have presented a facsimile, a masterpiece. At the great exhibition in Venice years ago the portrait of a mongoloid was displayed: the subject was *très dégoûtant*, but why not? Art can justify everything. Expect that upon approaching it, one discovered that it was not a portrait but the unfortunate himself, in flesh and blood. The experiment was then interrupted *manu militari*, but in a strictly theoretical context it was completely justified. For many years critics with university chairs had preached the absolute necessity of the death of art, waiting for who knows what palingenesis or resurrection, of which the signs could not be glimpsed.

What conclusion can be drawn from such facts? Evidently the arts, all the visual arts, are becoming more democratic in the worst sense of the word. Art is the production of objects for consumption, to be used and discarded while waiting for a new world in which man will have succeeded in freeing himself of everything, even of his own consciousness. The example I cite could be extended to the exclusively noisy and undifferentiated music listened to in those places where millions of young people gather to exorcize the horror of their solitude. But why more than ever has civilized man reached the point of having horror of himself?

Obviously I foresee the objections. We must not bring in the illnesses of society, which have perhaps always existed, but were little known because the former means of communication did not permit us to know and diagnose the illness. It alarms me that a sort of general Doomsday atmosphere accom-panies an ever more wide-spread comfort, that well-being (there where it exists, that is in limited areas of the world) has the livid features of desperation. Against the dark background of this contemporary civilization of well-being, even the arts tend to mingle, to lose their identity. Mass communication, radio, and especially television, have attempted, not without success, to annihilate every possibility of solitude and reflection. Time becomes more rapid, works of a few years ago seem "dated" and the need the artist has to be listened to sooner or later becomes a spasmodic need of the topical, of the immediate. Whence the new art of our time which is the spectacle, a not necessarily theatrical exhibition in which the rudiments of every art are present and which effects a kind of psychic massage on the spectator or listener or reader as the case may be. The *deus ex machina* of this new heap is the director. His purpose is not only to co-ordinate scenic arrangements, but to give intentions to works which have none or have had other ones. There is a great sterility in all this, an immense lack of confidence in life. In such a landscape of hysterical exhibitionism what can be place of poetry, the most discrete of arts, be? So-called lyrical poetry is work, the fruit of solitude and accumulated impressions. This is still true today but in rather limited cases. We have however more numerous cases in which the self-proclaimed poet falls into step with new times. Poetry then becomes acoustic and visual. The words splash in all directions, like the explosion of a grenade, there is no true meaning, but a verbal earthquake with many epicenters. Decipherment is not necessary, in many cases the aid of the psychoanalyst may help. Since the visual aspect prevails, the poem becomes translatable, and this is a new phenomenon in the history of esthetics. This does not mean that the new poets are schizoid. Some of them can write classically traditional verse and pseudo-verses devoid of any sense. There is also poetry written to be shouted in a square in front of an enthusiastic crowd. This occurs especially in countries where authoritarian regimes are in power. And such athletes of poetic vocalism are not always devoid of talent. I will cite such a case and I beg your pardon if it is also a case which concerns me personally. But the fact, if it is true, demon-strates that by now there exist two types of poetry in cohabitation, one of which is for immediate consumption and dies as soon as it is expressed, while the other can sleep quietly. One day it will awaken, if it has the strength to do so.

True poetry is similar to certain pictures whose owner is unknown and which only a few initiated people know. However, poetry does not live solely in books or in school anthologies. The poet does not know and often will never know his true receiver. I will give you a personal example. In the archives of Italian newspapers there are the obituary articles for men who are still alive and active. These articles are called "crocodiles". A few years ago at the *Corriere della Sera* I discovered my "crocodile", signed by Taulero Zulberti, critic, translator and polyglot. He states that the great poet Majakovsky, having read one or more of my poems translated into Russian, said: "Here is a poet I like. I would like to be able to read him in Italian." The episode is not improbable. My first verses began go circulate in 1925 and Majakovsky (who travelled in the United States and elsewhere as well) committed suicide in 1930.

Majakovsky was a poet with a pantograph, with a megaphone. If he said such words I can say that my poems had found, by crooked and unforeseeable paths, their receiver.

Do not believe, however, that I have a solipsistic idea of poetry. The idea of writing for the so-called happy few was never mine. In reality art is always for everyone and for no one. But what remains unforeseeable is its true begetter, its receiver. Spectacle-art, mass art, art which wants to produce a sort of physical-psychical message on a hypothetical user, has ·infinite

roads in front of it because the population of the world is in continuous
growth. But its limit is absolute void. It is possible to frame and exhibit
a pair of slippers (I myself have seen mine in that condition), but a landscape,
a lake or any great natural spectacle cannot be displayed under glass.

Lyrical poetry has certainly broken its barriers. There is poetry even in
prose, in all the great prose which is not merely utilitarian or didactic: there
exist poets who write in prose or at least in more or less apparent prose;
millions of poets write verses which have no connection with poetry. But
this signifies little or nothing. The world is growing, no one can say what
its future will be. But it is not credible that mass culture, with its ephemeral
and brittle character, will not produce, through necessary repercussions, a
culture which is both defense and reflection. We can all collaborate in this
future. But man's life is short and the life of the world can be almost infinitely
long.

I had thought of giving this title to my short speech: "Will poetry be able
to survive in the universe of mass communication?" That is what many people
wonder, but upon thinking closely, the answer can only be affirmative.
If by poetry one means belletristic poetry it is clear that the world
production will continue to grow excessively. If instead we limit ourselves
to that poetry which refuses with horror the description of production,
that which arises almost through a miracle and seems to embalm an entire
epoch and a whole linguistic and cultural situation, then it is necessary
to say that there is no death possible for poetry.

It has often been observed that the repercussion of poetic language on
prose language can be considered a decisive cut of a whip. Strangely,
Dante's *Divine Comedy* did not produce a prose of that creative height or
it did so after centuries. But if you study French prose before and after
the school of Ronsard, the Pléiade, you will observe that French prose has
lost that softness for which it was judged to be so inferior to the classical
languages and has taken a veritable leap towards maturity. The effect has
been curious. The Pléiade does not produce collections of homogeneous
poems like those of the Italian *dolce stil nuovo* (which is certainly one of
its sources), but it gives us from time to time true "antique pieces" which
could be put in a possible imaginary museum of poetry. It is a question
of a taste which could be defined as Neo-Greek and which centuries
later the Parnasse will attempt in vain to equal. This proves that great lyric
poetry can die, be reborn, die again, but will always remain one of the most
outstanding creations of the human soul. Let us reread together a poem
by Joachim Du Bellay. This poet, born in 1522 and who died at the age
of thirty-three, was the nephew of a Cardinal with whom he lived in Rome
for several years, bringing back a profound disgust for the corruption of
the papal court. Du Bellay wrote a great deal, imitating with greater or
lesser success the poets of the Petrarchan tradition. But the poem (perhaps
written in Rome), inspired by Latin verses by Navagero, which confirms
his fame, is the fruit of a painful nostalgia for the country-side of the sweet

Loire which he had abandoned. From Sainte-Beuve up to Walter Pater, who dedicated Joachim a memorable profile, the sort *Odelette* read it if this is possible, because it is a question of a poem in which the eye *des vanneurs de blé* has entered the repertory of world poetry. Let us try to reread it if this is possible. because it is a question of a poem in which the eye has its role.

A vous troppe legere,
qui d'aele passagere
par le monde volez
et d'un sifflant murmure
l'ombrageuse verdure
doulcement esbranlez,

j'offre ces violettes,
ces lis et ces fleurettes,
et ces roses icy,
ces vermeillettes roses,
tout freschement écloses,
et ces oeilletz aussi.

De vostre doulce halaine
eventez ceste plaine,
eventez ce sejour,
ce pendant que j'ahanne
a mon blé, que je vanne
a la chaleur du jour.

I do not if this *Odelette* was written in Rome as an interlude in the dispatch of boring office matters. It owes its current survival to Pater. At a distance of centuries a poem can find its interpreter.

But now in order to conclude, I should reply to the question which gave a title to this brief speech. In the current consumistic civilization which sees new nations and new languages appear in history, in the civilization of robot-man, what can the destiny of poetry be? There could be many answers. Poetry is the art which is technically within the grasp of everyone: a piece of paper and a pencil and one is ready. Only at a second moment do the problems of publishing and distribution arise. The fire of the library of Alexandria destroyed three fourths of Greek literature.

Today not even a universal fire could make the torrential poetic production of our time disappear. But it is exactly a question of production, that is, of hand-made products which are subject to the laws of taste and fashion. That the garden of the Muses can be devastated by great tempests is, more than probable, certain. But it seems to me just as certain that a great deal of printed paper and many books of poetry must resist time.

The question is different if one refers to the spiritual revival of an old poetic text, its contemporary restoration, its opening to new interpretations. And finally it always remains doubtful within which limits one moves when speaking of poetry. Much of today's poetry is expressed in prose. Many of today's verses are prose and bad prose. Narrative art, the novel, from Murasaki to Proust, has produced great works of poetry. And the theater? Many literary histories do not even discuss it, taking up instead several geniuses who are treated separately. In addition how can one explain the fact that ancient Chinese poetry survives all translations while European poetry is chained to its original language? Perhaps the phenomenon can be explained by the fact that we believe we are reading Po Chü-i and instead we are reading the wonderful counterfeiter Arthur Waly? One could multiply the questions with the sole result that not only poetry, but all the world of artistic expression or that which proclaims itself to be such, has entered into a crisis which is strictly tied to the human condition, to our existence as human beings, to our certainty or illusion of believing ourselves to be privileged beings, the only ones who believe they are the masters of their destiny and the depositaries of a destiny which no other creature can lay claim to. It is useless then to wonder what the destiny of the arts will be. It is like asking oneself if the man of tomorrow, perhaps of a very distant tomorrow, will be able to resolve the tragic contradictions in which he has been floundering since the first day of Creation (and if it is still possible to speak of such a day, which can be an endless epoch).

Literature 1976

SAUL BELLOW

"for the human understanding and subtle analysis of contemporary culture that are combined in his work"

THE NOBEL PRIZE FOR LITERATURE

Speech by KARL RAGNAR GIEROW, of the Swedish Academy
Translation from the Swedish text

Your Majesties, Your Royal Highnesses, Ladies and Gentlemen,
When Saul Bellow published his first book, the time had come for a change
of climate and generation in American narrative art. The so-called hard-boiled
style, with its virile air and choppy prose, had now slackened into an everyday
routine, which was pounded out automatically; its rigid paucity of words left
not only much unsaid but also most of it unfelt, unexperienced. Bellow's first
work, *Dangling Man* (1944), was one of the signs portending that something
else was at hand.

In Bellow's case emancipation from the previous ideal style took place in
two stages. In the first he reached back to the kind of perception that had
found its already classic guides in Maupassant, Henry James and Flaubert
perhaps most of all. The masters he followed expressed themselves as re-
strainedly as those he turned his back on. But the emphasis was elsewhere.
What gave a story its interest was not the dramatic, sometimes violent action
but the light it shed over the protagonist's inner self. With that outlook the
novel's heroes and heroines could be regarded, seen through and exposed, but
not glorified. The anti-hero of the present was already on the way, and
Bellow became one of those who took care of him.

Dangling Man, the man without a foothold, was thus a significant watchword
to Bellow's writing and has to no small extent remained so. He pursued the
line in his next novel, *The Victim* (1947) and, years later, with mature mastery
in *Seize the Day* (1956). With its exemplary command of subject and form the
last-mentioned novel has received the accolade as one of the classic works of our
time.

But with the third story in this stylistically coherent suite, it is as if Bellow
had turned back in order at last to complete something which he himself had
already passed. With his second stage, the decisive step, he had already left
this school behind him, whose disciplined form and enclosed structure gave
no play to the resources of exuberant ideas, flashing irony, hilarious comedy
and discerning compassion which he also knew he possessed and whose scope
he must try out. The result was something quite new, Bellow's own mixture
of rich picaresque novel and subtle analysis of our culture, of entertaining
adventure, drastic and tragic episodes in quick succession, interspersed with
philosophic conversation with the reader—that too very entertaining—all
developed by a commentator with a witty tongue and penetrating insight into
the outer and inner complications that drive us to act or prevent us from acting
and that can be called the dilemma of our age.

First in the new phase came *The Adventures of Augie March* (1953). The very wording of the title points straight to the picaresque, and the connexion is perhaps most strongly in evidence in this novel. But here Bellow had found his style, and the tone recurs in the following series of novels that form the bulk of his work: *Henderson the Rain King* (1959), *Herzog* (1964), *Mr Sammler's Planet* (1970) and *Humboldt's Gift* (1975). The structure is apparently loose-jointed but for this very reason gives the author ample opportunity for descriptions of different societies; they have a rare vigour and stringency and a swarm of colourful, clearly defined characters against a background of carefully observed and depicted settings, whether it is the magnificent façades of Manhattan in front of the backyards of the slums and semi-slums, Chicago's impenetrable jungle of resourceful businessmen intimately intertwined with obliging criminal gangs, or the more literal jungle, in the depths of Africa, where the novel, *Henderson the Rain King*, the writer's most imaginative expedition, takes place. In a nutshell they are all stories on the move and, like the first book, are about a man with no foothold, but (and it is important to add this) a man who keeps on *trying to find* a foothold during his wanderings in our tottering world.

Even a few minutes' sketch of Bellow's many-sided writings should indicate where that foothold lies. It cannot be pointed out, as none of his protagonists reaches it. But during their escapades they are all on the run, not *from* something but *towards* something, a goal somewhere which will give them what they lack—firm ground under their feet. "I want, I want, I want!" Henderson exclaims, and sets off for an unknown continent. What his demands are he does not know; what he demands is to find out, and his own desire is the unknown continent. "A worthwhile fate," Augie March calls his goal. And Herzog, the restless seeker after truth, for his part tries out one phrasing after the other of what he means by "a worthwhile fate". At one point he says confidently that "the realm of facts and that of value are not eternally separated". The words are uttered in passing but are worth dwelling on, and if we think of them as coming from Bellow himself they are essential. Giving value a place side by side with palpable facts is, as regards literature, a definite departure from realism. As a philosophy it is a protest against the determinism that must make man unaccountable for his actions as well as inert or hostile to life, since it prevents him from feeling, choosing and acting himself. The awareness of a value, on the other hand, gives man freedom, thereby responsibility, thereby a desire for action and a faith in the future. That is why Bellow, never one to look through rose-coloured spectacles, is at heart an optimist. It is the light of that conviction which makes the facets of his writing sparkle. His "anti-heroes" are victims of constant disappointment, born to defeat without end, and Bellow (it cannot be over-emphasized) loves and is able to transform the fate they find worthwhile into superb comedies. But they triumph nonetheless, they are heroes nonetheless, since they never give up the realm of values in which man becomes human. And, as Augie March says, anyone can become alive to this fact at any moment, however unfortunate he may be, "if he will be quiet and wait it out".

The realm of facts and that of value—the very combination of words is reminiscent of a work by the philosopher Wolfgang Köhler, professor first at Göttingen, then in Berlin, finally at Princeton, to which he fled from the Nazis. Köhler's book is called *The Place of Value in a World of Facts* and lent its name to an international Nobel symposium in Stockholm some years ago, at which a lecture was given by E. H. Gombrich, disciple and younger friend of Köhler. He told of the latter's last night in Berlin, before the flight could be carried out. Köhler spent the slow hours with like-minded friends, and while they waited, wondering if a patrol would clamp up the stairs at the last moment and pound on the door with rifle butts, they played chamber music. "Such is," Gombrich remarked, "the place of value in a world of facts".

The threatened position of value between obtrusive realities has not escaped Bellow; that is what he is always writing about. But he does not think that either mankind's conduct or the explosive development of the sciences betoken a world catastrophe. He is an optimist-in-spite-of-all, and thus also an opposition leader of human kindness. Truth must out, of course. But it is not always hostile. Facing the truth is not necessarily the same as braving death. "There may be truths on the side of life," he has said. "There may be some truths which are, after all, our friends in the universe."

In an interview once Bellow described something of what happens when he writes. Most of us, he supposed, have a primitive prompter or commentator within, who from earliest years has been telling us what the real world is. He himself has such a commentator in him; he has to prepare the ground for him and take notice of what he says. One is put in mind of another man who went out into the highways and byways with his questions, taking notice of his inner voice: Socrates and his daemon. This introspective listening demands seclusion. As Bellow himself puts it, "Art has something to do with the achievement of stillness in the midst of chaos. A stillness which characterizes prayer, too, and the eye of the storm." This was what prevailed when Köhler played chamber music on his last night in Berlin while, aware of imminent disaster, "being quiet and waiting it out". It is there that the value and dignity of life and mankind have their sole haven, ever storm-lashed, and it is from that stillness that Saul Bellow's work, borne on the whirlwind of disquiet, derives its inspiration and strength.

Dear Mr Bellow, it is my task and my great pleasure to convey to you the warm congratulations of the Swedish Academy and to ask you to receive from the hands of His Majesty the King the Nobel Prize for Literature of the year 1976.

Saul Bellow

SAUL BELLOW

Saul Bellow was born in Lachine, Quebec, a suburb of Montreal, in 1915, and was raised in Chicago. He attended the University of Chicago, received his Bachelor's degree from Northwestern University in 1937, with honors in sociology and anthropology, did graduate work at the University of Wisconsin, and served in the Merchant Marine during World War II.

Mr. Bellow's first novel, *Dangling Man*, was published in 1944, and his second, *The Victim*, in 1947. In 1948 he was awarded a Guggenheim Fellowship and spent two years in Paris and traveling in Europe, where he began *The Adventures of Augie March*, which won the National Book Award for fiction in 1954. Later books include *Seize The Day* (1956), *Henderson The Rain King* (1959), *Herzog* (1964), *Mosby's Memoirs and Other Stories* (1968), and *Mr. Sammler's Planet* (1970). His most recent work of fiction, *Humboldt's Gift* (1975), was awarded the Pulitzer Prize. Both *Herzog* and *Mr. Sammler's Planet* were awarded the National Book Award for fiction. Mr. Bellow's first non-fiction work, *To Jerusalem and Back: A Personal Account*, published on October 25, 1976, is his personal and literary record of his sojourn in Israel during several months in 1975.

In 1965 Mr. Bellow was awarded the International Literary Prize for *Herzog*, becoming the first American to receive the prize. In January 1968 the Republic of France awarded him the Croix de Chevalier des Arts et Lettres, the highest literary distinction awarded by that nation to non-citizens, and in March 1968 he received the B'nai B'rith Jewish Heritage Award for "excellence in Jewish literature", and in November 1976 he was awarded the America's Democratic Legacy Award of the Anti-Defamation League of B'nai B'rith, the first time this award has been made to a literary personage.

A playwright as well as a novelist, Saul Bellow is the author of *The Last Analysis* and of three short plays, collectively entitled *Under the Weather*, which were produced on Broadway in 1966. He has contributed fiction to *Partisan Review*, *Playboy*, *Harper's Bazaar*, *The New Yorker*, *Esquire*, and to literary quarterlies. His criticism has appeared in *The New York Times Book Review*, *Horizon*, *Encounter*, *The New Republic*, *The New Leader*, and elsewhere. During the 1967 Arab-Israeli conflict, he served as a war correspondent for *Newsday*. He has taught at Bard College, Princeton University, and the University of Minnesota, and is a member of the Committee on Social Thought at the University of Chicago.

Further works:

To Jerusalem and Back. A Personal Account, 1976
Him with His Foot in his Mouth and Other Stories, 1984
More Die of Heartbreak. A Novel, 1987
The Bellarosa Connection. A Novella, 1989
A Theft (novella), 1989
Something to Remember Me By. Three Tales, 1992

NOBEL LECTURE

December 12, 1976
by SAUL BELLOW
USA

I was a very contrary undergraduate more than 40 years ago. It was my habit to register for a course and then to do most of my reading in another field of study. So that when I should have been grinding away at "Money and Banking" I was reading the novels of Joseph Conrad. I have never had reason to regret this. Perhaps Conrad appealed to me because he was like an American—he was an uprooted Pole sailing exotic seas, speaking French and writing English with extraordinary power and beauty. Nothing could be more natural to me, the child of immigrants who grew up in one of Chicago's immigrant neighborhoods of course!—a Slav who was a British sea captain and knew his way around Marseilles and wrote an Oriental sort of English. But Conrad's *real* life had little oddity in it. His themes were straightforward— fidelity, command, the traditions of the sea, hierarchy, the fragile rules sailors follow when they are struck by a typhoon. He believed in the strength of these fragile-seeming rules, and in his art. His views on art were simply stated in the preface to *The Nigger of the Narcissus*. There he said that art was an attempt to render the highest justice to the visible universe: that it tried to find in that universe, in matter as well as in the facts of life, what was fundamental, enduring, essential. The writer's method of attaining the essential was different from that of the thinker or the scientist. These, said Conrad, knew the world by systematic examination. To begin with the artist had only himself; he descended within himself and in the lonely regions to which he descended, he found "the terms of his appeal". He appealed, said Conrad, "to that part of our being which is a gift, not an acquisition, to the capacity for delight and wonder . . . our sense of pity and pain, to the latent feeling of fellowship with all creation—and to the subtle but invincible conviction of solidarity that knits together the loneliness of innumerable hearts . . . which binds together all humanity—the dead to the living and the living to the unborn."

This fervent statement was written some 80 years ago and we may want to take it with a few grains of contemporary salt. I belong to a generation of readers that knew the long list of noble or noble-sounding words, words like "invincible conviction" or "humanity" rejected by writers like Ernest Hemingway. Hemingway spoke for the soldiers who fought in the First World War under the inspiration of Woodrow Wilson and other rotund statesmen whose big words had to be measured against the frozen corpses of young men paving the trenches. Hemingway's youthful readers were convinced that the horrors of the 20th Century had sickened and killed humanistic beliefs with their deadly radiations. I told myself, therefore, that Conrad's rhetoric must be resisted. But I never thought him mistaken. He spoke directly to me. The feeling individual appeared weak—he felt nothing but his own weakness. But if he accepted his weakness and his separateness and descended into himself intensifying his loneliness, he discovered his solidarity with other isolated creatures.

I feel no need now to sprinkle Conrad's sentences with skeptical salt. But there are writers for whom the Conradian novel—all novels of that sort—are gone forever. Finished. There is, for instance, M. Alain Robbe-Grillet, one of the leaders of French literature, a spokesman for "thingism"—*choseisme*. He writes that in great contemporary works, Sartre's *Nausea*, Camus' *The Stranger*, or Kafka's *The Castle*, there are no characters; you find in such books not individuals but—well, entities. "The novel of characters," he says, "belongs entirely in the past. It describes a period: that which marked the apogee of the individual." This is not necessarily an improvement; that Robbe-Grillet admits. But it is the truth. Individuals have been wiped out. "The present period is rather one of administrative numbers. The world's destiny has ceased, for us, to be identified with the rise and fall of certain men of certain families." He goes on to say that in the days of Balzac's bourgeoisie it was important to have a name and a character; character was a weapon in the struggle for survival and success. In that time, "It was something to have a face in a universe where personality represented both the means and the end of all exploration." But our world, he concludes, is more modest. It has renounced the omnipotence of the person. But it is more ambitious as well, "since it looks beyond. The exclusive cult of the 'human' has given way to a larger consciousness, one that is less anthropocentric." However, he comforts us, a new course and the promise of new discoveries lie before us.

On an occasion like this I have no appetite for polemics. We all know what it is to be tired of "characters". Human types have become false and boring. D. H. Lawrence put it early in this century that we human beings, our instincts damaged by Puritanism, no longer care for, were physically repulsive to one another. "The sympathetic heart is broken," he said. He went further, "We stink in each other's nostrils." Besides, in Europe the power of the classics has for centuries been so great that every country has its "identifiable personalities" derived from Molière, Racine, Dickens or Balzac. An awful phenomenon. Perhaps this is connected with the wonderful French saying. "*S'il y a un caractère, il est mauvais.*" It leads one to think that the unoriginal human race tends to borrow what it needs from convenient sources, much as new cities have often been made out of the rubble of old ones. Then, too, the psychoanalytic conception of character is that it is an ugly rigid formation—something we must resign ourselves to, not a thing we can embrace with joy. Totalitarian ideologies, too, have attacked bourgeois individualism, sometimes identifying character with property. There is a hint of this in M. Robbe-Grillet's argument. Dislike of personality, bad masks, false being have had political results.

But I am interested here in the question of the artist's priorities. Is it necessary, or good, that he should begin with historical analysis, with ideas or systems? Proust speaks in *Time Regained* of a growing preference among young and intelligent readers for works of an elevated analytical, moral or sociological tendency. He says that they prefer to Bergotte (the novelist in *Remembrance of Things Past*) writers who seem to them more profound. "But," says Proust, "from the moment that works of art are judged by reasoning, nothing is stable or certain, one can prove anything one likes."

The message of Robbe-Grillet is not new. It tells us that we must purge ourselves of bourgeois anthropocentricism and do the classy things that our advanced culture requires. Character? "Fifty years of disease, the death notice signed many times over by the serious essayists," says Robbe-Grillet, "yet nothing has managed to knock it off the pedestal on which the 19th century had placed it. It is a mummy now, but one still enthroned with the same phony majesty, among the values revered by traditional criticism."

The title of Robbe-Grillet's essay is *On Several Obsolete Notions*. I myself am tired of obsolete notions and of mummies of all kinds but I never tire of reading the master novelists. And what is one to do about the characters in their books? Is it necessary to discontinue the investigation of character? Can anything so vivid in them now be utterly dead? Can it be that human beings are at a dead end? Is individuality really so dependent on historical and cultural conditions? Can we accept the account of those conditions we are so "authoritatively" given? I suggest that it is not in the intrinsic interest of human beings but in these ideas and accounts that the problem lies. The staleness, the inadequacy of these repels us. To find the source of trouble we must look into our own heads.

The fact that the death notice of character "has been signed by the most serious essayists" means only that another group of mummies, the most respectable leaders of the intellectual community, has laid down the law. It amuses me that these serious essayists should be allowed to sign the death notices of literary forms. Should art follow culture? Something has gone wrong.

There is no reason why a novelist should not drop "character" if the strategy stimulates him. But it is nonsense to do it on the theoretical ground that the period which marked the apogee of the individual, and so on, has ended. We must not make bosses of our intellectuals. And we do them no good by letting them run the arts. Should they, when they read novels, find nothing in them but the endorsement of their own opinions? Are we here on earth to play such games?

Characters, Elizabeth Bowen once said, are not created by writers. They pre-exist and they have to be *found*. If we do not find them, if we fail to represent them, the fault is ours. It must be admitted, however, that finding them is not easy. The condition of human beings has perhaps never been more difficult to define. Those who tell us that we are in an early stage of universal history must be right. We are being lavishly poured together and seem to be experiencing the anguish of new states of consciousness. In America many millions of people have in the last forty years received a "higher education"— in many cases a dubious blessing. In the upheavals of the Sixties we felt for the first time the effects of up-to-date teachings, concepts, sensitivities, the pervasiveness of psychological, pedagogical, political ideas.

Every year we see scores of books and articles which tell the Americans what a state they are in—which make intelligent or simpleminded or extravagant or lurid or demented statements. All reflect the crises we are in while telling us what we must do about them; these analysts are produced by the very disorder and confusion they prescribe for. It is as a writer that I am considering their extreme moral sensitivity, their desire for perfection, their intolerance of the defects of society, the touching, the comical boundlessness of their demands, their anxiety, their irritability, their sensitivity, their tender-mindedness, their goodness, their convulsiveness, the recklessness with which they experiment with drugs and touch-therapies and bombs. The ex-Jesuit Malachi Martin in his book on the Church compares the modern American to Michelangelo's sculpture, *The Captive*. He sees "an unfinished struggle to emerge whole" from a block of matter. The American "captive" is beset in his struggle by "interpretations, admonitions, forewarnings and descriptions of himself by the self-appointed prophets, priests, judges and prefabricators of his travail," says Martin.

Let me take a little time to look more closely at this travail. In private life, disorder or near-panic. In families—for husbands, wives, parents, children—confusion; in civic behavior, in personal loyalties, in sexual practices (I will not recite the whole list; we are tired of hearing it)—further confusion. And with this private disorder goes public bewilderment. In the papers we read what used to amuse us in science fiction—*The New York Times* speaks of death rays and of Russian and American satellites at war in space. In the November *Encounter* so sober and responsible an economist as my colleague, Milton Friedman, declares that Great Britain by its public spending will soon go the way of poor countries like Chile. He is appalled by his own forecast. What — the source of that noble tradition of freedom and democratic rights that began with Magna Carta ending in dictatorship? "It is almost impossible for anyone brought up in that tradition to utter the word that Britain is in danger of losing freedom and democracy; and yet it is a fact!"

It is with these facts that knock us to the ground that we try to live. If I were debating with Professor Friedman I might ask him to take into account the resistance of institutions, the cultural differences between Great Britain and Chile, differences in national character and traditions, but my purpose is not to get into debates I can't win but to direct your attention to the terrible predictions we have to live with, the background of disorder, the visions of ruin.

You would think that one such article would be enough for a single number of a magazine but on another page of *Encounter* Professor Hugh Seton-Watson discusses George Kennan's recent survey of American degeneracy and its dire meaning for the world. Describing America's failure, Kennan speaks of crime, urban decay, drug-addiction, pornography, frivolity, deteriorated educational standards and concludes that our immense power counts for nothing. We cannot lead the world and, undermined by sinfulness, we may not be able to defend ourselves. Professor Seton-Watson writes, "Nothing can defend a society if its upper 100,000 men and women, both the decision-makers and those who help to mould the thinking of the decision-makers, are resolved to capitulate."

So much for the capitalist superpower. Now what about its ideological adversaries? I turn the pages of *Encounter* to a short study by Mr. George Watson, Lecturer in English at Cambridge, on the racialism of the Left. He tells us that Hyndman, the founder of the Social Democratic Federation, called the South African war the Jews' war; that the Webbs at times expressed racialist views (as did Ruskin, Carlyle and T. H. Huxley before them); he relates that Engels denounced the smaller Slav peoples of Eastern Europe as counter-revolutionary ethnic trash; and Mr. Watson in conclusion cites a public statement by Ulrike Meinhof of the West German "Red Army Faction" made at a judicial hearing in 1972 approving of "revolutionary extermination". For her, German anti-semitism of the Hitler period was essentially anti-capitalist. "Auschwitz," she is quoted as saying, "meant that six million Jews were killed and thrown on the waste heap of Europe for what they were: money Jews (Geldjuden)."

I mention these racialists of the Left to show that for us there is no simple choice between the children of light and the children of darkness. Good and evil are not symmetrically distributed along political lines. But I have made my point; we stand open to all anxieties. The decline and fall of everything is our daily dread, we are agitated in private life and tormented by public questions.

And art and literature—what of them? Well, there is a violent uproar but we are not absolutely dominated by it. We are still able to think, to discriminate, and to feel. The purer, subtler, higher activities have not succumbed to fury or to nonsense. Not yet. Books continue to be written and read. It may be more difficult to reach the whirling mind of a modern reader but it is possible to cut through the noise and reach the quiet zone. In the quiet zone we may find that he is devoutly waiting for us. When complications increase, the desire for essentials increases too. The unending cycle of crises that began with the First World War has formed a kind of person, one who has lived through terrible, strange things, and in whom there is an observable shrinkage of prejudices, a casting off of disappointing ideologies, an ability to live with many kinds of madness, an immense desire for certain durable human goods—truth, for instance, or freedom, or wisdom. I don't think I am exaggerating; there is plenty of evidence for this. Disintegration? Well, yes. Much is disintegrating but we are experiencing also an odd kind of refining process. And this has been going on for a long time. Looking into Proust's *Time Regained* I find that he was clearly aware of it. His novel, describing French society during the Great War, tests the strength of his art. Without art, he insists, shirking no personal or collective horrors, we do not know ourselves or anyone else. Only art penetrates what pride, passion, intelligence and habit erect on all sides—the seeming realities of this world. There is another reality, the genuine one, which we lose sight of. This other reality is always sending us hints, which, without art, we can't receive. Proust calls these hints our "true impressions." The true impressions, our persistent intuitions, will, without art, be hidden from us and we will be left with nothing but a "terminology for practical ends which we falsely call life." Tolstoy put the matter in much the same way. A book like his *Ivan Ilyitch* also describes these same "practical ends" which conceal both life and death from us. In his final sufferings Ivan Ilyitch becomes an individual, a "character", by tearing down the concealments, by seeing through the "practical ends."

Proust was still able to keep a balance between art and destruction, insisting that art was a necessity of life, a great independent reality, a magical power. But for a long time art has not been connected, as it was in the past, with the main enterprise. The historian Edgar Wind tells us in *Art and Anarchy* that Hegel long ago observed that art no longer engaged the central energies of man. These energies were now engaged by science—a "relentless spirit of rational inquiry." Art had moved to the margins. There it formed "a wide and splendidly varied horizon." In an age of science people still painted and wrote poetry but, said Hegel, however splendid the gods looked in modern works of art and whatever dignity and perfection we might find "in the images of God the Father and the Virgin Mary" it was of no use: we no longer bent our knees. It is a long time since the knees were bent in piety. Ingenuity, daring exploration, freshness of invention replaced the art of "direct relevance." The most significant achievement of this pure art, in Hegel's view, was that, freed from its former responsibilities, it was no longer "serious." Instead it raised the soul through the "serenity of form above any painful involvement in the limitations of reality." I don't know who would make such a claim today for an art that raises the soul above painful involvements with reality. Nor am I sure that at this moment, it is the spirit of rational inquiry in pure science that engages the central energies of man. The center seems (temporarily perhaps) to be filled up with the crises I have been describing.

There were European writers in the 19th-Century who would not give up the connection of literature with the main human enterprise. The very suggestion would have shocked Tolstoy and Dostoevski. But in the West a separation between great artists and the general public took place. They developed a marked contempt for the average reader and the bourgeois mass. The best of them saw clearly enough what sort of civilization Europe had produced, brilliant but unstable, vulnerable, fated to be overtaken by catastrophe, the historian Erich Auerbach tells us. Some of these writers, he says, produced "strange and vaguely terrifying works, or shocked the public by paradoxical and extreme opinions. Many of them took no trouble to facilitate the understanding of what they wrote—whether out of contempt for the public, the cult of their own inspiration, or a certain tragic weakness which prevented them from being at once simple and true."

In the 20th Century, theirs is still the main influence, for despite a show of radicalism and innovation our contemporaries are really very conservative. They follow their 19th-Century leaders and hold to the old standard, interpreting history and society much as they were interpreted in the last century. What would writers do today if it would occur to them that literature might once again engage those "central energies", if they were to recognize that an immense desire had arisen for a return from the periphery, for what was simple and true?

Of course we can't come back to the center simply because we want to; but the fact that we are wanted might matter to us and the force of the crisis is so great that it may summon us back to such a center. But prescriptions are futile. One can't tell writers what to do. The imagination must find its own path. But one can fervently wish that they—that we—would come back from the periphery. We do not, we writers, represent mankind adequately. What account do Americans give of themselves, what accounts of them are given by psychologists, sociologists, historians, journalists, and writers? In a kind of contractual daylight they see themselves in the ways with which we are so desperately familiar. These images of contractual daylight, so boring to Robbe-Grillet and to me, originate in the contemporary world view: We put into our books the consumer, civil servant, football fan, lover, television viewer. And in the contractual daylight version their life is a kind of death. There is another life coming from an insistent sense of what we are which denies these daylight formulations and the false life—the death in life—they make for us. For it is false, and we know it, and our secret and incoherent resistance to it cannot stop, for that resistance arises from persistent intuitions. Perhaps humankind cannot bear too much reality, but neither can it bear too much unreality, too much abuse of the truth.

We do not think well of ourselves; we do not think amply about what we are. Our collective achievements have so greatly "exceeded" us that we "justify" ourselves by pointing to them. It is the jet plane in which we commonplace human beings have crossed the Atlantic in four hours that embodies such value as we can claim. Then we hear that this is closing time in the gardens of the West, that the end of our capitalist civilization is at hand. Some years ago Cyril Connolly wrote that we were about to undergo "a complete mutation, not merely to be defined as the collapse of the capitalist system, but such a sea-change in the nature of reality as could not have been envisaged by Karl Marx or Sigmund Freud." This means that we are not yet sufficiently shrunken; we must prepare to be smaller still. I am not sure whether this should be called intellectual analysis or analysis by an intellectual. The disasters are disasters. It would be worse than stupid to call them victories as some statesmen have tried to do. But I am drawing attention to the fact that there is in the intellectual community a sizeable inventory of attitudes that have become respectable— notions about society, human nature, class, politics, sex, about mind, about the physical universe, the evolution of life. Few writers, even among the best, have taken the trouble to re-examine these attitudes or orthodoxies. Such attitudes only glow more powerfully in Joyce or D. H. Lawrence than in the books of lesser men; they are everywhere and no one challenges them seriously. Since the Twenties, how many novelists have taken a second look at D. H. Lawrence, or argued a different view of sexual potency or the effects of industrial civilization on the instincts? Literature has for nearly a century used the same stock of ideas, myths, strategies. "The most serious essayists of the last fifty years," says Robbe-Grillet. Yes, indeed. Essay after essay, book after book, confirm the most serious thoughts—Baudelairian, Nietzschean, Marxian, Psychoanalytic, etcetera, etcetera—of these most serious essayists. What Robbe-Grillet says about character can be said also about these ideas, maintaining all the usual things about mass society, dehumanization and the rest. How weary we are of them. How poorly they represent us. The pictures they offer no more resemble us than we resemble the reconstructed reptiles and other monsters in a museum of paleontology. We are much more limber, versatile, better articulated, there is much more to us, we all feel it.

What is at the center now? At the moment, neither art nor science but mankind determining, in confusion and obscurity, whether it will endure or go under. The whole species—everybody—has gotten into the act. At such a time it is essential to lighten ourselves, to dump encumbrances, including the encumbrances of education and all organized platitudes, to make judgments of our own, to perform acts of our own. Conrad was right to appeal to that part of our being which is a gift. We must hunt for that under the wreckage of many systems. The failure of those systems may bring a blessed and necessary release from formulations, from an over-defined and misleading consciousness. With increasing frequency I dismiss as merely respectable opinions I have long held—or thought I held—and try to discern what I have really lived by, and what others live by. As for Hegel's art freed from "seriousness" and glowing on the margins, raising the soul above painful involvement in the limitations of reality through the serenity of form, that can exist nowhere now, during this struggle for survival. However, it is not as though the people who engaged in this struggle had only a rudimentary humanity, without culture, and knew nothing of art. Our very vices, our mutilations, show how rich we are in thought and culture. How much we know. How much we even feel. The struggle that convulses us makes us want to simplify, to reconsider, to eliminate the tragic weakness which prevented writers—and readers—from being at once simple and true.

Writers are greatly respected. The intelligent public is wonderfully patient with them, continues to read them and endures disappointment after disappointment, waiting to hear from art what it does not hear from theology, philosophy, social theory, and what it cannot hear from pure science. Out of the struggle at the center has come an immense, painful longing for a broader, more flexible, fuller, more coherent, more comprehensive account of what we human beings are, who we are, and what this life is for. At the center humankind struggles with collective powers for its freedom, the individual struggles with dehumanization for the possession of his soul. If writers do not come again into the center it will not be because the center is pre-empted. It is not. They are free to enter. If they so wish.

The essence of our real condition, the complexity, the confusion, the pain of it is shown to us in glimpses, in what Proust and Tolstoy thought of as "true impressions". This essence reveals, and then conceals itself. When it goes away it leaves us again in doubt. But we never seem to lose our connection with the depths from which these glimpses come. The sense of our real powers, powers we seem to derive from the universe itself, also comes and goes. We are reluctant to talk about this because there is nothing we can prove, because our language is inadequate and because few people are willing to risk talking about it. They would have to say, "There is a spirit" and that is taboo. So almost everyone keeps quiet about it, although almost everyone is aware of it.

The value of literature lies in these intermittent "true impressions". A novel moves back and forth between the world of objects, of actions, of appearances, and that other world from which these "true impressions" come and which moves us to believe that the good we hang onto so tenaciously—in the face of evil, so obstinately—is no illusion.

No one who has spent years in the writing of novels can be unaware of this. The novel can't be compared to the epic, or to the monuments of poetic drama. But it is the best we can do just now. It is a sort of latter-day lean-to, a hovel in which the spirit takes shelter. A novel is balanced between a few true impressions and the multitude of false ones that make up most of what we call life. It tells us that for every human being there is a diversity of existences, that the single existence is itself an illusion in part, that these many existences signify something, tend to something, fulfill something; it promises us meaning, harmony and even justice. What Conrad said was true, art attempts to find in the universe, in matter as well as in the facts of life, what is fundamental, enduring, essential.

Literature 1977

VICENTE ALEIXANDRE

"for a creative poetic writing which illuminates man's condition in the cosmos and in present-day society, at the same time representing the great renewal of the traditions of Spanish poetry between the wars"

THE NOBEL PRIZE FOR LITERATURE

Speech by Dr. KARL RAGNAR GIEROW, of the Swedish Academy
Translation from the Swedish text

Your Majesties, Your Royal Highnesses, Ladies and Gentlemen,
This year's Nobel prizewinner in literature, Vicente Aleixandre, is hard to
understand and in one way controversial. The latter may be due to the
former. For even his devoted admirers offer varying interpretations of his
poetry. It is doubtful if anyone has yet been able to sum it up properly, one
reason being that fifty years after Aleixandre's début his writing still seems
to be forging ahead. His two most remarkable collections of poems, the twin
crowns of his career to date, appeared in 1968 *(Poemas de la consumación)*
and 1974 *(Diálogos del conocimiento)*.

On one point, however, all are agreed: Aleixandre's place and importance
in the spiritual life of Spain. In the history of literature he is part of the
current that broke into Spanish poetry in the 1920s with unequalled breadth
and force. One of the names of the vigorous avantgarde was the Pleiades.
It is all the more suitable as no one with the naked eye can make out the
correct number in the group of stars that we colloquially call The Seven
Sisters. There are many more of them, and in the firmament of Spanish
poetry these Pleiades are usually numbered at around twenty-five—a brilliant
cluster of lyric talent. Among those who came to shine the brightest and the
longest is Vicente Aleixandre.

The affinity of the new style with French surrealism is striking. There are
those in Spain who prefer to call it apparent. They are sometimes reluctant
to stress the points in common, asserting their unconformity all the more
strongly. The Spanish declaration of independence is not without ground.
The Second Golden Age, which is another name for the breakthrough and
epoch of the Pleiades, referred directly and expressly to the first, Spain's
century-long age of greatness, the baroque. When the young guard banded
together to strike their big blow they chose as a standard to celebrate the
300th anniversary of Luis de Góngora, the creator of the hair-splitting
"estilo culto" who originated and gave his name to the ingeniously and
extravagantly ornamented gongorism. Virtuose pastiches on Spanish baroque
poetry in frills, and beside them folksong variations of rustic themes, were
characteristic elements in the renewal during the 1920s south of the Pyre-
nees, and they distinguish it undeniably from the manifestos up by the Seine.

When this vital generation of poets, with Lorca at the head, stormed the
Spanish Parnassus, Aleixandre too was busy with his pen. He was then
writing about the need of rationalization and pension and insurance problems
on the Spanish railways, where he was employed. But in 1925 something
happened which was to determine the whole of his existence and still does

today. He was taken seriously ill with renal tuberculosis. It changed his life in two ways. He had to leave his employment and he could take another position with communications of a different kind: those of poetry. When the Góngora anniversary was celebrated he had not yet published his first volume of verse, but he had printed poems in the Pleiades' magazines and was already a member of the group. He was perhaps the one least concerned about the connexion with "the golden century" and to that extent also the one who came closest to the new doctrines from Paris. This may be the background to a somewhat defiant declaration by one of his poet friends that Spanish surrealism had given French surrealism what it had always lacked—a great poet: Vicente Aleixandre. But he has never been a mediator in this literary frontier dispute. Against the basic article of faith "l'écriture automatique" he has reiterated his belief in "la conciencia creadora", creative consciousness. He went his own way.

In extremely simplified terms it is the way from a cosmic vision to a realistic close-up. One of Aleixandre's conclusive collections of poems is called *La destrucción o el amor* (Destruction or Love). The title is thematically pregnant with meaning and certain Aleixandre connoisseurs have taken it to mean an *Either-Or,* to quote Kierkegaard: without love all that is left to us is destruction. But the word "or" can mean not only two alternative contrasts but also an explanatory addition, and what the title then says is: Destruction, in other words love. It would agree better with the perspective of creation in its entirety that these poems, and those that followed, aim at depicting and that Aleixandre has been striving for ever since his début with *Ambito.* "Man is an element in the cosmos and in his being does not differ from it", as he himself says. Love *is* destruction, but destruction is a result of or an act of love, of self-effacement, of man's innate yearning to be received back into the world order from which, as a living being, he has been separated and cast out—"segregado—degradado". His decease therefore has nothing of despair at a meaningful life meeting with a meaningless death. Only with death does life acquire its meaning and is complete; it is the last birth, *Nacimiento último,* as one of the later collections of poems is called. Aleixandre does not hesitate to carry his vision to the paradoxical extreme: "Man does not exist." In other words: so long as he is alive, he is actually unborn.

But out of the conviction that man is an element in a cosmic whole grows of necessity the awareness that our short life on earth is also a part of the same course of events. It is that knowledge which has brought Aleixandre back to "the tellurian world", as he calls it, given his continued writings a proximity to life, an openness and directness which formerly he was not capable of or did not strive for, and has made his last two books, mentioned in the introduction to this presentation, the peak of his work hitherto. On his way there, but conscious of where he was heading, he wrote in *Historia del corazón* a poem called *Entre dos oscuridades un relámpago,* A Lightning Between Two Darknesses. In it is the earth, in it is man, and life must be affirmed so long as we have it. Intentionally or not one of the gifted dreamers of our time here quotes the words of another visionary when the meaning of the play is to be explained:

"We are such stuff as dreams are made on,
and our little life is rounded with a sleep."

Outwardly too Aleixandre went his own way. When the civil war came he was bedridden and listened to the bombs exploding. Lorca was murdered, other poet friends died in prison, and when the remainder went into exile at the end of the war, a constellation scattered to the four winds, they had to leave the invalid behind. But mentally as well Aleixandre survived the régime. He never submitted to it and went on with his writing, frail but unbroken, thereby becoming the rallying-point and source of power in Spain's spiritual life that we today have the pleasure of honouring.

The Swedish Academy deeply regrets that owing to his state of health Mr Aleixandre can't be here today. But as his representative we greet his friend and younger colleague, Mr Justo Jorge Padron, and I ask you, Mr Padrón, to convey to Mr Aleixandre our warmest congratulations and to receive the Nobel Prize for Literature, awarded to him, from the hands of His Majesty the King.

VICENTE ALEIXANDRE

Vicente Aleixandre was born in Sevilla (Spain) on April 26, 1898. He spent his childhood in Malaga and he has lived in Madrid since 1909. Studied law at the University of Madrid and at the Madrid School of Economics. Beginning in 1925 he has completely devoted himself to literature. His first book of poems, *Ambit*, appeared in 1928. Since that date he has written and published a score of books. In 1933, he received the National Literary Prize for his work *Destruction or Love*. He spent the Civil War in the Republican zone. He fell ill and remained in Madrid at the end of the conflict, silenced by the new authorities for four years. In 1944, he published *The Shadow of Paradise*, still maintaining his independence of the established political situation. In 1950, he became a member of the Spanish Academy. His books and anthologies have been published up to the present day. The Swedish Academy awarded him the Nobel Prize for Literature for the totality of his work in 1977.

Further works:
Sonido de la guerra/ Sound of War (poetry), 1978
Epistolario/ Letters, 1986

Vicente Aleixandre died in 1984.

NOBEL LECTURE
December 12, 1977
by
VICENTE ALEIXANDRE
SPAIN
Translation

At a moment like this, so important in the life of a man of letters, I should like to express in the most eloquent words at my command the emotion that a human being feels and the gratitude he experiences in the face of an event such as that which is taking place today. I was born in a middle-class family, but I had the benefit of its eminently open and liberal outlook. My restless spirit led me to practise contradictory professions. I was a teacher of mercantile law, an employee in a railway company, a financial journalist. From early youth this restlessness of which I have spoken lifted me to one particular delight: reading and, in time, writing. At the age of 18 the prentice poet began to write his first verses, sketched out in secret amid the turmoil of a life which, because it had not yet found its true axis, I might call adventurous. The destiny of my life, its direction, was determined by a bodily weakness. I became seriously ill of a chronic complaint. I had to abandon all my other concerns, those which I might call corporal, and to retreat to the countryside far from my former activities. The vacuum thus created was soon invaded by another activity which did not call for physical exertion and could easily be combined with the rest that the doctors had ordered me to take. This unforgettable, all-conquering invasion was the practice of letters; poetry occupied to the full the gap in activity. I began to write with complete dedication and it was then, only then, that I became possessed by the passion which was never to leave me.

Hours of solitude, hours of creation, hours of meditation. Solitude and meditation gave me an awareness, a perspective which I have never lost: that of solidarity with the rest of mankind. Since that time I have always proclaimed that poetry is communication, in the exact sense of that word.

Poetry is a succession of questions which the poet constantly poses. Each poem, each book is a demand, a solicitation, an interrogation, and the answer is tacit, implicit, but also continuous, and the reader gives it to himself through his reading. It is an exquisite dialogue in which the poet questions and the reader silently gives his full answer.

I wish I could find fitting words to describe what a Nobel prize means to the poet. It cannot be done; I can only assure you that I am with you body and soul, and that the Nobel prize is as it were the response, not gradual, not tacit, but collected and simultaneous, sudden, of a general voice which generously and miraculously becomes one and itself answers the unceasing question which it has come to address to mankind. Hence my gratitude for this symbol of the collected and simultaneous voice to which the Swedish Academy has enabled me to listen with the senses of the soul for which I here publicly render my devoted thanks.

On the other hand, I consider that a prize such as I have received today is, in all circumstances, and I believe without exception, a prize directed to the literary tradition in which the author concerned—in this case myself—has been formed. For there can be no doubt that poetry, art, are always and above all tradition, and in that tradition each individual author represents at most a modest link in the chain leading to a new kind of aesthetic expression; his fundamental mission is, to use a different metaphor, to pass on a living torch to the younger generation which has to continue the arduous struggle. We can conceive of a poet who has been born with the highest talents to accomplish a destiny. He will be able to do little or nothing unless he has the good fortune to find himself placed in an artistic current of sufficient strength and validity. Conversely, I think that a less gifted poet may perhaps play a more successful role if he is lucky enough to be able to develop himself within a literary move-ment which is truly creative and alive. In this respect I was born under the protection of benign stars inasmuch as, during a sufficiently long period be-fore my birth, Spanish culture had undergone an extremely important process of swift renewal, a development which I think is no secret to anyone. Novelists such as Galdós; poets like Machado, Unamuno, Juan Ramón Jiménez and, earlier, Becquer; philosophers like Ortega y Gasset; prose writers such as Azorín and Baroja; dramatists such as Valle-Inclán; painters like Picasso and Miró; composers such as de Falla: such figures do not just conjure themselves up, nor are they the products of chance. My generation saw itself aided and en-riched by this warm environment, by this source, by this enormously fertile cultural soil, without which perhaps none of us would have become anything.

From the tribune in which I now address you I should like therefore to associate my words with this generous nursery ground of my compatriots who from another era and in the most diverse ways formed us and enabled us, myself and my friends of the same generation, to reach a place from which we could speak with a voice which perhaps was genuine or was peculiar to our-selves.

And I do not refer only to these figures which constitute the immediate tradition, which is always the one most visible and determinative. I allude also to the other tradition, the one of the day before yesterday, which though more distant in time was yet capable of establishing close ties with ourselves; the tradition formed by our classics from the Golden Age, Garcilaso, Fray Luis de León, San Juan de la Cruz, Gongora, Quevedo, Lope de Vega, to which we have also felt linked and from which we have received no little stimulation. Spain was able to revive and renew herself thanks to the fact that, through the generation of Galdós, and later through the generation of 1898, she as it were opened herself, made herself available, and as a result of this the whole of the nourishing sap from the distant past came flowing towards us in overwhelming abundance. The generation of 1927 did not wish to spurn anything of the great deal that remained alive in this splendid world of the past which suddenly lay revealed to our eyes in a lightning flash of uninterrupted beauty. We rejected nothing, except what was mediocre; our generation tended to-wards affirmation and enthusiasm, not to scepticism or taciturn restraint.

Everything that was of value was of interest to us, no matter whence it came. And if we were revolutionaries, if we were able to be that, it was because we had once loved and absorbed even those values against which we now reacted. We supported ourselves firmly on them in order to brace ourselves for the perilous leap forward to meet our destiny. Thus it should not surprise you that a poet who began as a surrealist today presents a defence of tradition. Tradition and revolution—here are two words which are identical.

And then there was the tradition, not vertical but horizontal, which came to help us in the form of a stimulating and fraternal competition from our flanks, from the side of the road we were pursuing. I refer to that other group of young people (when I too was young) who ran with us in the same race. How fortunate I was to be able to live and perform, to mould myself in the company of poets so admirable as those I came to know and devote myself to with the right of a contemporary! I loved them dearly, every one. I loved them precisely because I was seeking something different, something which it was only possible to find through differences and contrast in relation to these poets, my comrades. Our nature achieves its true individuality only in community with others, face to face with our neighbours. The higher the quality of the human environment in which our personality is formed, the better it is for us. I can say that here, too, I have had the good fortune to be able to realize my destiny through communion with one of the best companies of men of which it is possible to conceive. The time has come to name this company in all its multiplicity: Federico García Lorca, Rafael Alberti, Jorge Guillén, Pedro Salinas, Manuel Altolaguirre, Emilio Prados, Dámaso Alonso, Gerardo Diego, Luis Cernuda.

I speak then of solidarity, of communion, as well as of contrast. If I do so, it is becauce such has been the feeling that has been most deeply implanted on my soul, and it is its heartbeat. that, in one way or another, can be heard most clearly behind the greater part of my verse. It is therefore natural that the very way in which I look upon humanity and poetry has much to do with this feeling. The poet, the truly determinative poet, is always a revealer; he is, essentially, a seer, a prophet. But his "prophecy" is of course not a prophecy about the future; for it may have to do with the past: it is a prophecy without time. Illuminator, aimer of light, chastiser of mankind, the poet is the possessor of a Sesame which in a mysterious way is, so to speak, the word of his destiny.

To sum up, then, the poet is a man who was able to be more than a man: for he is in addition a poet. The poet is full of "wisdom"; but this he cannot pride himself on, for perhaps it is not his own. A power which cannot be explained, a spirit, speaks through his mouth: the spirit of his race, of his peculiar tradition. He stands with his feet firmly planted on the ground, but 'beneath the soles of his feet a mighty current gathers and is intensified, flowing through his body and finding its way out through his tongue. Then it is the earth itself, the deep earth, that flames from his glowing body. But at other times the poet has grown, and now towards the heights, and with his brow reaching into the heavens, he speaks with a starry voice, with cosmic resonance, while he feels the very wind from the stars fanning his breast. All is then brotherhood and communion. The tiny ant, the soft blade of grass against which his cheek sometimes rests, these are not distinct from himself. And he can understand them and spy out their secret sound, whose delicate note can be heard amidst the rolling of the thunder.

I do not think that the poet is primarily determined by his goldsmith's work. Perfection in his work is something which he hopes gradually to achieve, and his message will be worth nothing if he offers mankind a coarse and inadequate surface. But emptiness cannot be covered up by the efforts of a polisher, however untiring he may be.

Some poets—this is another problem and one which does not concern expression but the point of departure—are poets of "minorities". They are artists (how great they are does not matter) who owe their individuality to devoting themselves to exquisite and limited subjects, to refined details (how delicate and profound were the poems that Mallarmé devoted to fans!), to the minutely savoured essences in individuals expressive of our detail-burdened civilization.

Other poets (here, too, their stature is of no importance) turn to what is enduring in man. Not to that which subtly distinguishes but to that which essentially unites. And even though they see man in the midst of the civilization of his own times, they sense all his pure nakedness radiating immutably from beneath his tired vestments. Love, sorrow, hate or death are unchanging. These poets are radical poets and they speak to the primary, the elemental in man. They cannot feel themselves to be the poets of "minorities". Among them I count myself.

And therefore a poet of my kind has what I would call a communicative vocation. He wants to make himself heard from within each human breast, since his voice is in a way the voice of the collective, the collective to which the poet for a moment lends his passionate voice. Hence the necessity of being understood in languages other than his own. Poetry can only in part be translated. But from this zone of authentic interpretation the poet has the truly extraordinary experience of speaking in another way to other people and being understood by them. And then something unexpected occurs: the reader is installed, as through a miracle, in a culture which in large measure is not his own but in which he can nevertheless feel without difficulty the beating of his own heart, which in this way communicates and lives in two dimensions of reality: its own and that conferred on it by the new home in which it has been received. What has been said remains equally true if we turn it round and apply it not to the reader but to the poet who has been translated into another language. The poet, too, feels himself to be like one of those figures encountered in dreams, which exhibit, perfectly identified, two distinct personalities. Thus it is with the translated author, who feels within himself two personæ: the one conferred on him by the new verbal attire which now covers him and his own genuine personæ which, beneath the other, still exists and asserts itself.

Thus I conclude by claiming for the poet a role of symbolic representation, enshrining as he does in his own person that longing for solidarity with humankind for which precisely the Nobel Prize was founded.

Literature 1978

ISAAC BASHEVIS SINGER

"for his impassioned narrative art which, with roots in a Polish-Jewish cultural tradition, brings universal human conditions to life"

THE NOBEL PRIZE FOR LITERATURE

Speech by Professor LARS GYLLENSTEN, of the Swedish Academy
Translation from the Swedish text

Your Majesties, Your Royal Highnesses, Ladies and Gentlemen,

"Heaven and earth conspire that everything which has been, be rooted
out and reduced to dust. Only the dreamers, who dream while awake, call
back the shadows of the past and braid from unspun threads, unspun
nets." These words from one of Isaac Bashevis Singer's stories in the
collection *The Spinoza of Market Street* (1961) say quite a lot about the writer
himself and his narrative art.

Singer was born in a small town or village in eastern Poland and grew up
in one of the poor, over-populated Jewish quarters of Warsaw, before and
during the First World War. His father was a rabbi of the Hasid school of
piety, a spiritual mentor for a motley collection of people who sought his
help. Their language was Yiddish – the language of the simple people and
of the mothers, with its sources far back in the middle ages and with an
influx from several different cultures with which this people had come in
contact during the many centuries they had been scattered abroad. It is
Singer's language. And it is a storehouse which has gathered fairytales and
anecdotes, wisdom, superstitions and memories for hundreds of years past
through a history that seems to have left nothing untried in the way of
adventures and afflictions. The Hasid piety was a kind of popular Jewish
mysticism. It could merge into prudery and petty-minded, strict adherence
to the law. But it could also open out towards orgiastic frenzy and messian-
ic raptures or illusions.

This world was that of East-European Jewry – at once very rich and very
poor, peculiar and exotic but also familiar with all human experience
behind its strange garb. This world has now been laid waste by the most
violent of all the disasters that have overtaken the Jews and other people in
Poland. It has been rooted out and reduced to dust. But it comes alive in
Singer's writings, in his waking dreams, his very waking dreams, clear-
sighted and free of illusion but also full of broad-mindedness and unsenti-
mental compassion. Fantasy and experience change shape. The evocative
power of Singer's inspiration acquires the stamp of reality, and reality is
lifted up by dreams and imagination into the sphere of the supernatural,
where nothing is impossible and nothing is sure.

Singer began his writing career in Warsaw in the years between the wars.
Contact with the secularized environment and the surging social and
cultural currents involved a liberation from the setting in which he had
grown up – but also a conflict. The clash between tradition and renewal,
between other-worldliness and pious mysticism on the one hand and free

thought, doubt and nihilism on the other, is an essential theme in Singer's short stories and novels. Among many other themes, it is dealt with in Singer's big family chronicles — the novels *The Family Moskat, The Manor* and *The Estate,* from the 1950s and 1960s. These extensive epic works depict how old Jewish families are broken up by the new age and its demands and how they are split, socially and humanly. The author's apparently inexhaustible psychological fantasy and insight have created a microcosm, or rather a well-populated micro-chaos, out of independent and graphically convincing figures.

Singer's earliest fictional works, however, were not big novels but short stories and novellas. The novel *Satan in Goray* appeared in 1935, when the Nazi terror was threatening and just before the author emigrated to the USA, where he has lived and worked ever since. It treats of a theme to which Singer has often returned in different ways — the false Messiah, his seductive arts and successes, the mass hysteria around him, his fall and the breaking up of illusions in destitution and new illusions or in penance and purity. *Satan in Goray* takes place in the 17th century after the cruel ravages of the Cossacks with outrages and mass murder of Jews and others. The book anticipates what was to come in *our* time. These people are not wholly evil, not wholly good — they are haunted and harassed by things over which they have no control, by the force of circumstances and by their own passions — something alien but also very close.

This is typical of Singer's view of humanity — the power and fickle inventiveness of obsession, the destructive but also inflaming and creative potential of the emotions and their grotesque wealth of variation. The passions can be of the most varied kinds — often sexual but also fanatical hopes and dreams, the figments of terror, the lure of lust or power, the nightmares of anguish. Even boredom can become a restless passion, as with the main character in the tragicomic picaresque novel *The Magician of Lublin* (1961), a kind of Jewish Don Juan and rogue, who ends up as an ascetic or saint. In a sense a counterpart to this book is *The Slave* (1962), really a legend of a lifelong, faithful love which becomes a compulsion, forced into fraud despite its purity, heavy to bear though sweet, saintly but with the seeds of shamefulness and deceit. The saint and the rogue are near of kin.

Singer has perhaps given of his best as a consummate storyteller and stylist in the short stories and in the numerous and fantastic novellas, available in English translation in about a dozen collections. The passions and crazes are personified in these strange tales as demons, spectres and ghosts, all kinds of infernal or supernatural powers from the rich store-house of Jewish popular belief or of his own imagination. These demons are not only graphic literary symbols but also real, tangible forces. The middle ages seem to spring to life again in Singer's works, the daily round is interwoven with wonders, reality is spun from dreams, the blood of the past pulsates in the present. This is where Singer's narrative art celebrates its greatest triumphs and bestows a reading experience of a deeply original kind, harrowing but also stimulating and edifying. Many of his characters step with unquestioned authority into the Pantheon of literature where the eternal companions and mythical figures live, tragic and grotesque, comic and touching, weird and wonderful − people of dream and torment, baseness and grandeur.

Dear Mr. Singer, master and magician! It is my task and my great pleasure to convey to you the heartiest congratulations of the Swedish Academy and to ask you to receive from the hands of His Majesty the King the Nobel Prize for Literature 1978.

ISAAC BASHEVIS SINGER

In one of his more light-hearted books Isaac Bashevis Singer depicts his childhood in one of the over-populated poor quarters of Warsaw, a Jewish quarter, just before and during the First World War. The book, called *In My Father's Court* (1966), is sustained by a redeeming, melancholy sense of humour and a clear-sightedness free of illusion. This world has gone for-ever, destroyed by the most terrible of all scourges that have afflicted the Jews and other people in Poland. But it comes to life in Singer's memories and writing in general. Its mental and physical environment and its centur-ies-old traditions have set their stamp on Singer as a man and a writer and provide the ever-vivid subject matter for his inspiration and imagination. It is the world and life of East-European Jewry, such as it was lived in cities and villages, in poverty and persecution, and imbued with sincere piety and rites combined with blind faith and superstition. Its language was Yiddish – the language of the simple people and of the women, the lan-guage of the mothers, preserved fairytales and anecdotes, legends and memories of hundreds of years through a history which seems to have left nothing untried in the way of agony, passions, aberrations, cruelty and bestiality but also of heroism, love and self-sacrifice.

Singer's father was a rabbi, a spiritual mentor and confessor of the Hasid school of piety. His mother also came from a family of rabbis. The East-European, Jewish-mystical Hasidism combined Talmud doctrine and a fidelity to scripture and rites – which often merged into prudery and strict adherence to the law – with a lively and sensually candid earthiness that seemed familiar with all human experience. Its world, which the reader encounters in Singer's stories, is a very Jewish but also a very human world. It appears to include everything – pleasure and suffering, coarseness and subtlety. We find obtrusive carnality, spicy, colourful, fragrant or smelly, lewd or violent. But there is also room for sagacity, worldly wisdom and shrewd speculation. The range extends from the saintly to the demoniacal, from quiet contemplation and sublimity to ruthless obsession and infernal confusion or destruction. It is typical that among the authors Singer read at an early age who have influenced him and accompanied him through life, were Spinoza, Gogol and Dostoevsky, in addition to Talmud, Cabala and kindred writings.

Singer began his writing career as a journalist in Warsaw in the years between the wars. He was influenced by his elder brother, now dead, who was already an author and who contributed to the younger brother's spiritual liberation and contact with the new currents of seething political, social and cultural upheaval. The clash between tradition and renewal, between other-worldliness and faith and mysticism on the one hand, and free thought, secularization, doubt and nihilism on the other, is an essential theme in Singer's short stories and novels. The theme is Jewish, made topical by the barbarous conflicts of our age, a painful drama between contentious loyalties. But it is also of concern to mankind, to us all, Jew or non-Jew, actualized by modern western culture's struggles between preservation and renewal. Among many other themes, it is dealt with in Singer's big family chronicles—the novels *The Family Moskat* (1950), *The Manor* (1967) and *The Estate* (1969). These extensive epic works have been compared with Thomas Mann's novel *Buddenbrooks*. Like Mann, Singer describes how old families are broken up to the new age and its demands, from the middle of the 19th Century up to the Second World War, and how they are split financially, socially and humanly. But Singer's chronicles are greater in scope than Mann's novel and more richly orchestrated in their characterization. The author's apparently inexhaustible fantasy has created a microcosm, or rather a well-populated microchaos, out of independent and graphically convincing figures. They bring to mind another writer whom Singer read when young—Leo Tolstoy.

Singer's earliest fictional works, however, were not big novels but short stories and novellas, a genre in which he has perhaps given of his very best as a consummate storyteller and stylist. The novel *Satan in Goray,* written originally in Yiddish like practically all Singer's books, appeared in 1935, when the Nazi catastrophe was threatening and just before the author emigrated to the USA, where he has lived and worked ever since. It treats of a theme to which Singer has often returned in different ways and with variations in time, place and personages—the false Messiah, his seductive arts and successes, the mass hysteria around him, his fall and the breaking up of illusions in destitution and new illusions or in penance and purity. *Satan in Goray* takes place in the 17th Century, in the period of confusion and through sufferings after the cruel ravages of the Cossacks outrages and mass murder of Jews, peasants and artisans. The people in this novel, as in other works by Singer, are often at the mercy of capricious circumstance but even more of their own passions. The passions are frequently of a sexual nature but also of another kind—manias and superstitions, fanatical hopes and dreams, the figments of terror, the lure of lust or power, the nightmares of anguish, and so on. Even boredom can become a restless passion, as with the main character in the tragicomic picaresque novel *The Magician of Lublin* (1961), a most eccentric antihero, a kind of Jewish Don Juan and rogue, who ends up as an ascetic or saint.

This is one of the most characteristic themes with Singer—the tyranny of the passions, the power and fickle inventiveness of obsession, the grotesque wealth of variation and the destructive but also inflaming and paradoxically creative potential of the emotions. We encounter this tumultuous and colourful world particularly in Singer's numerous and fantastic short stories, available in English translation in about a dozen collections, from the early *Gimpel The Fool* (translated 1953) to the later work *A Crown of Feathers* (1973), with notable masterpieces in between, such as *The Spinoza of Market Street* (1961) or *A Friend of Kafka* (1970). The passions and crazes are personified in Singer as demons, spectres, ghosts and all kinds of infernal or supernatural powers from the rich storehouse of Jewish popular imagination. These demons are not only graphic literary symbols but also real, tangible beings – Singer in fact says he believes in their physical presence. The middle ages rise up in his work and permeate the present. Everyday life is interwoven with wonders, reality with dreams, the blood of the past with the moment in which we are living. This is where Singer's narrative art celebrates its greatest triumphs and bestows a reading experience of a deeply original kind, harrowing but also stimulating and edifying. Many of his characters step with unquestioned authority into the Pantheon of literature where the eternal companions and mythical figures live, tragic and grotesque, comic and touching, weird and wonderful – people of dream and torment, baseness and grandeur.

Books:
Issac Bashevis Singer, born in Radzymin near Warsaw, emigrated 1935 to USA. He died in 1991. In addition to the works mentioned above Singer's writings include – in English:

the novels
The Slave, transl. by the author and Cecil Hemley. New York: Farrar Straus, 1962; London: Secker and Warburg, 1963.
Enemies: A Love Story, transl. by Alizah Shevrin and Elizabeth Shub. N.Y.: Farrar Straus, 1972.
Shosha. N.Y.: Farrar Straus, 1978.
Reaches of Heaven. N.Y.: Farrar Straus, 1980.
The Golem. London: Deutsch, 1983.
The Penitent. N.Y.: Farrar Straus, 1983.
Yentl the Yeshiva Boy, transl. from the Yiddish by Marion Magid and Elisabeth Pollet. N.Y.: Farrar Straus, 1983.
The King of the Fields. N.Y.: Farrar Straus, 1988.
Scum, transl. by Rosaline Dukalsky Schwartz. N.Y.: Farrar Straus, 1991.

the collections of short stories
Short Friday, transl. by Ruth Whitman and others. N.Y.: Farrar Straus, 1964; London: Secker and Warburg, 1967.
The Séance, transl. by Ruth Whitman and others. N.Y.: Farrar Straus, 1968; London: Cape, 1970.
Passions, transl. by the author in collab. with others. N.Y.: Farrar Straus, 1975; London: Cape, 1976.
Old Love. N.Y.: Farrar Straus, 1979.
The Power of Light. N.Y.: Farrar Straus, 1980.
The Image and Other Stories. N.Y.: Farrar Straus, 1985.
The Death of Metuselah and Other Stories. London: Cape, 1988.

the memoirs
A Little Boy in Search of God: Mysticism in a Personal Light. N.Y.: Doubleday, 1976.
A Young Man in Search of Love, transl. by Joseph Singer. N.Y.: Doubleday, 1978.
Lost in America. N.Y.: Doubleday, 1981.

for children
Zlateh the Goat and Other Stories, transl. by the author and Elizabeth Shub. N.Y.: Harper, 1966; London: Secker and Warburg, 1967.
When Schlemiel Went to Warsaw and Other Stories, transl. by the author and Elizabeth Shub. N.Y.: Farrar Straus, 1968.

A Day of Pleasure: Stories of a Boy Growing up in Warsaw, transl. by the author and Elizabeth Shub. N.Y.: Farrar Straus, 1969.

The Fools of Chelm and Their History, transl. by the author and Elizabeth Shub. N.Y.: Farrar Straus, 1973.

Why Noah Chose the Dove, transl. by Elizabeth Shub. N.Y.: Farrar Straus, 1974.

Stories for Children. N.Y.: Farrar Straus, 1986.

NOBEL LECTURE

8 December, 1978
by
ISAAC BASHEVIS SINGER
USA

Ther storyteller and poet of our time, as in any other time, must be an entertainer of the spirit in the full sense of the word, not just a preacher of social or political ideals. There is no paradise for bored readers and no excuse for tedious literature that does not intrigue the reader, uplift him, give him the joy and the escape that true art always grants. Nevertheless, it is also true that the serious writer of our time must be deeply concerned about the problems of his generation. He cannot but see that the power of religion, especially belief in revelation, is weaker today than it was in any other epoch in human history. More and more children grow up without faith in God, without belief in reward and punishment, in the immortality of the soul and even in the validity of ethics. The genuine writer cannot ignore the fact that the family is losing its spiritual foundation. All the dismal prophecies of Oswald Spengler have become realities since the Second World War. No technological achievements can mitigate the disappointment of modern man, his loneliness, his feeling of inferiority, and his fear of war, revolution and terror. Not only has our generation lost faith in Providence but also in man himself, in his institutions and often in those who are nearest to him.

In their despair a number of those who no longer have confidence in the leadership of our society look up to the writer, the master of words. They hope against hope that the man of talent and sensitivity can perhaps rescue civilization. Maybe there is a spark of the prophet in the artist after all.

As the son of a people who received the worst blows that human madness can inflict, I must brood about the forthcoming dangers. I have many times resigned myself to never finding a true way out. But a new hope always emerges telling me that it is not yet too late for all of us to take stock and make a decision. I was brought up to believe in free will. Although I came to doubt all revelation, I can never accept the idea that the Universe is a physical or chemical accident, a result of blind evolution. Even though I learned to recognize the lies, the clichés and the idolatries of the human mind, I still cling to some truths which I think all of us might accept some day. There must be a way for man to attain all possible pleasures, all the powers and knowledge that nature can grant him, and still serve God — a God who speaks in deeds, not in words, and whose vocabulary is the Cosmos.

I am not ashamed to admit that I belong to those who fantasize that literature is capable of bringing new horizons and new perspectives — philosophical, religious, aesthetical and even social. In the history of old

Jewish literature there was never any basic difference between the poet and the prophet. Our ancient poetry often became law and a way of life.

Some of my cronies in the cafeteria near the Jewish Daily Forward in New York call me a pessimist and a decadent, but there is always a background of faith behind resignation. I found comfort in such pessimists and decadents as Baudelaire, Verlaine, Edgar Allan Poe, and Strindberg. My interest in psychic research made me find solace in such mystics as your Swedenborg and in our own Rabbi Nachman Bratzlaver, as well as in a great poet of my time, my friend Aaron Zeitlin who died a few years ago and left a literary inheritance of high quality, most of it in Yiddish.

The pessimism of the creative person is not decadence but a mighty passion for the redemption of man. While the poet entertains he continues to search for eternal truths, for the essence of being. In his own fashion he tries to solve the riddle of time and change, to find an answer to suffering, to reveal love in the very abyss of cruelty and injustice. Strange as these words may sound I often play with the idea that when all the social theories collapse and wars and revolutions leave humanity in utter gloom, the poet – whom Plato banned from his Republic – may rise up to save us all.

The high honor bestowed upon me by the Swedish Academy is also a recognition of the Yiddish language — a language of exile, without a land, without frontiers, not supported by any government, a language which possesses no words for weapons, ammunition, military exercises, war tactics; a language that was despised by both gentiles and emancipated Jews. The truth is that what the great religions preached, the Yiddish-speaking people of the ghettos practiced day in and day out. They were the people of The Book in the truest sense of the word. They knew of no greater joy than the study of man and human relations, which they called Torah, Talmud, Mussar, Cabala. The ghetto was not only a place of refuge for a persecuted minority but a great experiment in peace, in self-discipline and in humanism. As such it still exists and refuses to give up in spite of all the brutality that surrounds it. I was brought up among those people. My father's home on Krochmalna Street in Warsaw was a study house, a court of justice, a house of prayer, of storytelling, as well as a place for weddings and Chassidic banquets. As a child I had heard from my older brother and master, I. J. Singer, who later wrote *The Brothers Ashkenazi*, all the arguments that the rationalists from Spinoza to Max Nordau brought out against religion. I have heard from my father and mother all the answers that faith in God could offer to those who doubt and search for the truth. In our home and in many other homes the eternal questions were more actual than the latest news in the Yiddish newspaper. In spite of all the disenchantments and all my skepticism I believe that the nations can learn much from those Jews, their way of thinking, their way of bringing up children, their finding happiness where others see nothing but misery and humiliation. To me the Yiddish language and the conduct of those who spoke it are identical. One can find in the Yiddish tongue and in the Yiddish spirit expressions of pious joy, lust for life, longing for the Messiah, patience and deep appreciation of human individuality. There is a quiet humor in Yiddish and a gratitude for every day of life, every crumb of success, each encounter of love. The Yiddish mentality is not haughty. It does not take victory for granted. It does not demand and command but it muddles through, sneaks by, smuggles itself amidst the powers of destruction, knowing somewhere that God's plan for Creation is still at the very beginning.

There are some who call Yiddish a dead language, but so was Hebrew called for two thousand years. It has been revived in our time in a most remarkable, almost miraculous way. Aramaic was certainly a dead language for centuries but then it brought to light the Zohar, a work of mysticism of sublime value. It is a fact that the classics of Yiddish literature are also the classics of the modern Hebrew literature. Yiddish has not yet said its last word. It contains treasures that have not been revealed to the eyes of the world. It was the tongue of martyrs and saints, of dreamers and Cabalists — rich in humor and in memories that mankind may never forget. In a figurative way, Yiddish is the wise and humble language of us all, the idiom of frightened and hopeful Humanity.

Literature 1979

ODYSSEUS ELYTIS

"for his poetry, which, against the background of Greek tradition, depicts with sensuous strength and intellectual clear-sightedness modern man's struggle for freedom and creativeness"

THE NOBEL PRIZE FOR LITERATURE

Speech by Doctor KARL RAGNAR GIEROW, of the Swedish Academy. Translation from the Swedish text.

Your Majesties, Your Royal Highnesses, Ladies and Gentlemen,

When Giorgos Seferis, compatriot of this year's Nobel prizewinner in literature, came here in 1963 to receive the same award, he presented at the airport a bunch of hyacinths each to the then Secretary of the Swedish Academy and to its officiating director that winter as a greeting to their respective wives. He had picked them himself on Hymettus, the mountain a few miles east of Athens where Aphrodite had her miraculous spring and where, ever since antiquity, hyacinths grow wild in a profusion which makes the whole mountain smell of honey.

The episode comes naturally to mind now that we have the pleasure of welcoming Odysseus Elytis, the Greek writer who in his youth made his name with the collection *The Concert of Hyacinths,* in which he calls to his beloved: "Take with you the light of hyacinths and baptize it in the wellspring of day" and assures her that "when you glitter in the sun that on you glides waterdrops, and deathless hyacinths, and silences, I proclaim you the only reality."

But there is a more immediate reason today to think of the chivalrous gesture in the inhospitable sleet of the airport. The hyacinths Seferis gave us were not at all like those we are accustomed to see. And, freshly picked as they were, they became symbols not only of the climatic difference between the giver's sunny south and our snowy north. If Odysseus Elytis, the author of *The Concert of Hyacinths,* had wished to use that flower as one of the analogies between environment and perception that are an essential part of his cultural outlook, he could have said that our potplants are a west-European rationalization of something which in his country grows wild, thereby acquiring its everlasting beauty. To this beauty he has devoted most of what he has written, and a recurrent theme is the prevalent west-European misconception of all that goes to make up the distinctive world of ideas whose legitimate heir he is.

He has arrived at his critical view of our all too rationalistic picture of Greece, which he traces back to the Renaissance's ideal of antiquity, by his own familiarity with western Europe's poetry, art and way of thinking. It may seem like a paradox—one which he himself has pointed out—that it was this western Europe, branded by him for its sterile rationalism, which gave Elytis the impulse that all at once set free his own writing: surrealism, which cannot be said to exaggerate reason.

The paradox is, if not apparent, at any rate not entirely unusual. Like a rebellious pulse of exuberant life surrealism broke through the hardened arteries of calcified forms. Outside France too poetry was dominated by a school which called itself "Les Parnassiens" but which never reached even the foot of Parnassus, if we share Elytis's view of what Greece has been and still is. But also on the Greek Parnassus of that time sat the same connoisseurs of degeneration who, in ornate words, declared their pessimistic conviction that nothing in this world was worth anything except their ability to express perfectly this very thought. If such an atmosphere is to be called captivating, surrealism came as a liberation, a religious revival, even if the sign of the saved here and there was a mere speaking with tongues.

But much of the best that happens when an art form is rejuvenated is not the result of a definite program but the fruit of an unforeseen cross. For Greek poetry the contact with surrealism meant a flowering which allows us to call the last fifty years Hellas's second highwater mark. In none of the numerous important poets who have created this age of greatness can we see more clearly than in Elytis what this vigorous cross signified: the exciting meeting between epoch-making modernism and inherited myth.

A cursory presentation of a poet hard to understand should, then, first establish his relationship to these two components—surrealism and myth. The task is not as easy as it looks. We have his own word for it: "I considered surrealism," he says on the one hand, "as the last available oxygen in a dying world, dying, at least, in Europe." On the other hand he states definitely: "I never was a disciple of the surrealist school." Nor was he. Elytis will have nothing to do with its fundamental poetry, the automatic writing with its unchecked torrent of chance associations. His explorations in poetry's means of expression lead him to surrealism's antipodes. Even if its violent display of unproven combinations released his own writing, he is a man of strict form, the master of deliberate creation.

Read his *To Axion Estí*, by many regarded as his most representative work. With its painstaking composition and stately rhetoric it leaves not one syllable to chance. Or take his love poem *Monogram*, with its ingenious mathematical basis; it has few counterparts in the literature we know. It comprises seven songs, each with seven lines or multiples of seven in a rising scale 7−21−35 up to the middle song's culmination of 49, where the poem turns round and descends the staircase with exactly the same number of lines, 35−21−down to the final song's 7, the starting point. This is nothing that need worry the poem's readers; it has its beauty without our having to count its steps. But poetry with this structure like an Euclidean linear drawing does not take after surrealism's *écriture automatique*.

Elytis's relationship to the other component, to Greek myth, also calls for clarification. We are used to seeing Greece's treasure of myths melted down and remoulded to contemporary west-European patterns. We have an Antigone à la Racine, an Antigone à la Anouilh and we shall have more. For Elytis such treatment is odious, a rationalistic pot-cultivation of wildflowers. He himself writes no Antigone à la Breton. He imitates no myths at all and attacks those compatriots who do. In this world of ideas he also has his share of responsibility, though his writing is a repetition not of ancient tales from the Greek past but of the way in which myths are produced.

He sees his Greece with its glorious traditions, its mountains whose peaks with their very names remind us how high the human spirit has attained, and its waters the Aegean Sea, Elytis's home, whose waves for thousands of years have washed ashore the riches that the West has been able to gather in and pride itself on. For him this Greece is still a living, ever-active myth, and he depicts it just as the old mythmakers did, by personifying it and giving it human form. It lends a sensuous nearness to his visions, and the myth that is the creed of his poetry is incarnated by beautiful young people in an enchanting landscape who love life and each other in dazzling sunshine where the waves break on the shore.

We can call this an optimistic idealization and, despite the concreteness, a flight from the present moment and reality. Elytis's very language, ritually solemn, is constantly striving to get away from everyday life with its pettiness. The idealization explains both the rapture and the criticism that his poetry has aroused. Elytis himself has given his view of the matter, point by point. Greek as a language, he says, opposes a pessimistic description of life, and for *la poésie maudite* it has no expressions. For west-Europeans all mysticism is associated with the darkness and the night, but for the Greeks light is the great mystery and every radiant day its recurrent miracle. The sun, the sea and love are the basic and purifying elements.

Those who maintain that all true poetry must be a reflection of its age and a political act he can refer to his harrowing poem about the second lieutenant who fell in the Albanian war. Elytis, himself a second lieutenant, chanced to be one of the two officers who opened the secret order of general mobilization. He took part at the front in the passionate and hopeless fight against Mussolini's crushing superiority, and his lament over the fallen brother-in-arms, who personifies Greece's never-completed struggle for existence, is committed poetry in a much more literal and harsher sense than that familiar to those who usually clamour for literature's commitment.

Elytis's conclusions from his participation were of a different nature. The poet, he says, does not necessarily have to express his time. He can also heroically defy it. His calling is not to jot down items about our daily life with its social and political situations and private griefs. On the contrary, his only way leads "from what is to what may be". In its essence, therefore, Elytis's poetry is not logically clear as we see it but derives its light from the limpidity of the present moment against a perspective behind it. His myth has its roots by the Aegean Sea, which was his cradle, but the myth is about humanity, drawing its nourishment not from a vanished golden age but from one which can never be realized. It is pointless to call this either optimism or pessimism. For, if I have understood him aright, only our future is worth bearing in mind and the unattainable alone is worth striving for.

Cher Maître,

Malheureusement, mais sans doute au soulagement de l'auditoire, je ne parle pas votre langue. Pour employer la locution anglaise spécifique à quelque chose d'étrange : « It's Greek to me ». Mais votre poésie n'est certainement pas étrangère, portée par la mer, qui est en même temps la mère de la civilisation européenne. Dans cette descendance nous mettons notre gloire, et, par conséquent, il faut que je contredise votre diagnostic de notre état déplorable. Ce dont nous sommes atteints, ce n'est pas du tout d'un excès de rationalisme. Au contraire, la maladie de l'Europe occidentale c'est justement que le rationalisme est rationné. Et le peu que nous en détenons encore, ce ne sont pas les devoirs que nous ont donnés à apprendre nos philosophes de la renaissance. La sagesse claire et la logique pure de Platon et d'Aristote, peut-être aussi de Protagoras, de Gorgias et de Socrate lui-même, voilà les racines du rationalisme, dont nous ne voyons aujourd'hui que les épaves pitoyables.

Néanmoins Socrate, quand la raison ne lui donnait pas de gouverne, a écouté la voix de son daimon, et, cher maître, c'est avec une admiration très profonde que nous avons écouté se faire entendre en votre poésie la même voix de mystère, le daimon de votre pays.

J'ai grand plaisir à vous transmettre les félicitations les plus cordiales de l'Académie suédoise et à vous demander de recevoir des mains de Sa Majesté le Roi le Prix Nobel de littérature de cette année.

ODYSSEUS ELYTIS

Descendant of an old family of Lesbos, he was born in Heraclion (Candia) on the island of Crete, November 2, 1911. Some time later his family settled permanently in Athens where the poet finished his secondary school studies and later visited the Law School of the Athens University. His first appearance as a poet in 1935 through the magazine "Nea Grammata" ("New Culture") was saluted as an important event and the new style he introduced – though giving rise to a great many reactions – succeeded in prevailing and effectively contributing to the poetical reform commencing in the Second World War's eve and going on up to our days.

In 1937 he visited the Reserve Officer's Cadet School in Corfu. Upon the outbreak of the war he served in the rank of Second Lieutenant, first at the Headquarters of the 1st Army Corps and then at the 24th Regiment, on the advanced fire line. During the German occupation and later, after Greece was liberated, he has been unabatedly active, publishing successive collections of poetry and writing essays concerning contemporary poetry and art problems.

He has twice been Programme Director of the Greek National Radio Foundation (1945–46 and 1953–54), Member of the National Theatre's Administrative Council, President of the Administrative Council of the Greek Radio and Television Service as well as Member of the Consultative Committee of the Greek National Tourist's Organisation on the Athens Festival. In 1960 he was awarded the First State Poetry Prize, in 1965 the Order of the Phoenix Brigade and in 1975 he was proclaimed Doctor Honoris Causa of the Philosophical School of the Thessaloniki University and Honorary Citizen of the Town of Mytilene.

During the years 1948—1952 and 1969—1972 he settled in Paris. There, he listened to philology and literature lessons in the Sorbonne and got acquainted with the pioneers of the world's avant-garde (Reverdy, Breton, Tzara, Ungaretti, Matisse, Picasso, Chagall, Giacometti). Starting from Paris he travelled and visited subsequently Switzerland, England, Italy and Spain. In 1948 he was the representative of Greece at the "International Meetings of Geneva", in 1949 at the Founding Congress of the "International Art Critics Union" in Paris and in 1962 at the "Incontro Romano della Cultura" in Rome.

In 1961, upon an invitation of the State Department, he travelled through the U.S.A.; and – upon similar invitations – through the Soviet Union in 1963 and Bulgaria in 1965.

Elytis' poetry has marked, through an active presence of over forty years, a broad spectrum. Unlike others, he did not turn back to Ancient Greece or Byzantium but devoted himself exclusively to today's Hellenism, of which he attempted—in a certain way based on psychical and sentimental aspects—to build up the mythology and the institutions. His main endeavour has been to rid his people's conscience from remorses unjustifiable, to complement natural elements through ethical powers, to achieve the highest possible transparency in expression and to finally succeed in approaching the mystery of light, "the metaphysic of the sun"—according to his own definition. A parallel way concerning technique resulted in introducing the "inner architecture", which is clearly perceptible in a great many works of his; mainly in the *Axion Esti — It Is Worthy*. This work—thanks to its setting to music by Mikis Theodorakis—was to be widely spread among all Greeks and grew to be a kind of the people's new gospel. Elytis' theoretical ideas have been expressed in a series of essays under the title (*Offering*) *My Cards To Sight*. Besides he applied himself to translating poetry and theatre as well as creating a series of *collage* pictures. Translations of his poetry have been published as autonomous books, in anthologies or in periodicals in eleven languages.

Literature
"Orientations" (1940); "Sun – The First" (1943); "An Heroic And Funeral Chant For The Lieutenant Lost In Albania" (1946); "To Axion Esti" – "It Is Worthy" (1959); "Six Plus One Remorses For The Sky" (1960); "The Light Tree And The Fourteenth Beauty" (1972); "The Sovereign Sun" (1972); "The Trills Of Love" (1973); "The Monogram" (1973); "Step-Poems" (1974); "(Offering) My Cards To Sight" (1974); "The Painter Theophilos" (1973); "Second Writing" (1976); "The Magic Of Papadiamantis" (1976); "Signalbook" (1977); "Maria Nefeli" (1978); "Selected poems" Ed. E. Keeley and Ph. Sherrard (1981); "Three Poems under a Flag of Convenience" (1982); "Diary of an Invisible April" (1984); "The Little Mariner" (1988); "What I Love. Selected Poems" (1986); "Krinagoras" (1987); "The Elegies of Oxopetras" (1991).

Reference Works. Mario Vitti: Odysseus Elytis. Literature 1935–1971 (Icaros 1977); Tasos Lignadis: Elytis' Axion Esti (1972); Lili Zografos: Elytis - The Sun Drinker (1972); as well as the special issue of the American magazine Books Abroad dedicated to the work of Elytis (Autumn 1975. Norman, Oklahoma, U.S.A.); Odysseus Elytis: Anthologies of Light. Ed. I. Ivask (1981); A. Decavalles: Maria Nefeli and the Changeful Sameness of Elytis' Variations on a theme (1982); E. Keeley: Elytis and the Greek Tradition (1983); Ph. Sherrard: Odysseus Elytis and the Discovery of Greece, in Journal of Modern Greek Studies, 1(2), 1983; K. Malkoff: Eliot and Elytis: Poet of Time, Poet of Space, in Comparative Literature, 36(3), 1984; A. Decavalles: Odysseus Elytis in the 1980s, in World Literature Today, 62(1), 1988.

Translations. Poesie. Procedute dal Canto eroico e funebre per il sottotenente caduto in Albania. Trad. Mario Vitti (Roma. Il Presente. 1952); 21 Poesie. Trad. Vicenzo Rotolo (Palermo. Istituto Siciliano di Studi Bizantini e Neoellenici. 1968); Poèmes. Trad. Robert Levesque (1945); Six plus un remords pour le ciel. Trad. F. B. Mache (Fata Morgana. Montpellier 1977); Körper des Sommers. Übers. Barbara Schlörb (St. Gallen 1960); Sieben nächtliche Siebenzeiler. Übers. Günter Dietz (Darmstadt 1966); To Axion Esti - Gepriesen sei. Übers. Günter Dietz (Hamburg 1969); The Axion Esti. Trans. Edmund Keeley and G. Savidis (Pittsburgh, U.S.A. 1974); The Sovereign Sun. Trans. Kinom Friar (Philadelphia, U.S.A. 1974).

NOBEL LECTURE

December 8, 1979
By
ODYSSEUS ELYTIS
Greece
Translation

May I be permitted, I ask you, to speak in the name of luminosity and transparency. The space I have lived in and where I have been able to fulfill myself is defined by these two states. States that I have also perceived as being identified in me with the need to express myself.

It is good, it is right that a contribution be made to art, from that which is assigned to each individual by his personal experience and the virtues of his language. Even more so, since the times are dismal and we should have the widest possible view of things.

I am not speaking of the common and natural capacity of perceiving objects in all their detail, but of the power of the metaphor to only retain their essence, and to bring them to such a state of purity that their metaphysical significance appears like a revelation.

I am thinking here of the manner in which the sculptors of the Cycladic period used their material, to the point of carrying it beyond itself. I am also thinking of the Byzantine icon painters, who succeeded, only by using pure color, to suggest the "divine".

It is just such an intervention in the real, both penetrating and metamorphosing, which has always been, it seems to me, the lofty vocation of poetry. Not limiting itself to what is, but stretching itself to what can be. It is true that this step has not always been received with respect. Perhaps the collective neuroses did not permit it. Or perhaps because utilitarianism did not authorize men to keep their eyes open as much as was necessary.

Beauty, Light, it happens that people regard them as obsolete, as insignificant. And yet! The inner step required by the approach of the Angel's form is, in my opinion, infinitely more painful than the other, which gives birth to Demons of all kinds.

Certainly, there is an enigma. Certainly, there is a mystery. But the mystery is not a stage piece turning to account the play of light and shadow only to impress us.

It is what continues to be a mystery, even in bright light. It is only then that it acquires that refulgence that captivates and which we call

Beauty. Beauty that is an open path — the only one perhaps — towards that unknown part of ourselves, towards that which surpasses us. There, this could be yet another definition of poetry: the art of approaching that which surpasses us.

Innumerable secret signs, with which the universe is studded and which constitute so many syllables of an unknown language, urge us to compose words, and with words, phrases whose deciphering puts us at the threshold of the deepest truth.

In the final analysis, where is truth? In the erosion and death we see around us, or in this propensity to believe that the world is indestructible and eternal? I know, it is wise to avoid redundancies. The cosmogonic theories that have succeeded each other through the years have not missed using and abusing them. They have clashed among themselves, they have had their moment of glory, then they have been erased.

But the essential has remained. It remains.

The poetry that raises itself when rationalism has laid down its arms, takes its relieving troops to advance into the forbidden zone, thus proving that it is still the less consumed by erosion. It assures, in the purity of its form, the safeguard of those given facts through which life becomes a viable task. Without it and its vigilance, these given facts would be lost in the obscurity of consciousness, just as algae become indistinct in the ocean depths.

That is why we have a great need of transparency. To clearly perceive the knots of this thread running throughout the centuries and aiding us to remain upright on this earth.

These knots, these ties, we see them distinctly, from Heraclitus to Plato and from Plato to Jesus. Having reached us in various forms they tell us the same thing: that it is in the inside of this world that the other world is contained, that it is with the elements of this world that the other world is recombined, the hereafter, that second reality situated above the one where we live unnaturally. It is a question of a reality to which we have a total right, and only our incapacity makes us unworthy of it.

It is not a coincidence that in healthy times, Beauty is identified with Good, and Good with the Sun. To the extent that consciousness purifies itself and is filled with light, its dark portions retract and disappear, leaving empty spaces — just as in the laws of physics — are filled by the elements of the opposite import. Thus what results of this rests on the two aspects, I mean the "here" and the "hereafter". Did not Heraclitus speak of a harmony of opposed tensions?

It is of no importance whether it is Apollo or Venus, Christ or the Virgin who incarnate and personalize the need we have to see materialized what we experience as an intuition. What is important is the breath of immortality that penetrates us at that moment. In my humble opinion, Poetry should, beyond all doctrinal argumentation, permit this breath.

Here I must refer to Hölderlin, that great poet who looked at the gods of Olympus and Christ in the same manner. The stability he gave a kind of vision continues to be inestimable. And the extent of what he has revealed for us is immense. I would even say it is terrifying. It is what incites us to cry out — at a time when the pain now submerging us was just beginning—: "What good are poets in a time of poverty" Wozu Dichter in dürftiger Zeit?

For mankind, times were always dürftig, unfortunately. But poetry has never, on the other hand, missed its vocation. These are two facts that will never cease to accompany our earthly destiny, the first serving as the counter-weight to the other. How could it be otherwise? It is through the Sun that the night and the stars are perceptible to us. Yet let us note, with the ancient sage, that if it passes its bounds the Sun becomes "üßρις". For life to be possible, we have to keep a correct distance to the allegorical Sun, just as our planet does from the natural Sun. We formerly erred through ignorance. We go wrong today through the extent of our knowledge. In saying this I do not wish to join the long list of censors of our technological civilization. Wisdom as old as the country from which I come has taught me to accept evolution, to digest progress "with its bark and its pits".

But then, what becomes of Poetry? What does it represent in such a society? This is what I reply: poetry is the only place where the power of numbers proves to be nothing. Your decision this year to honor, in my person, the poetry of a small country, reveals the relationship of harmony linking it to the concept of gratuitous art, the only concept that opposes nowadays the all-powerful position acquired by the quantitative esteem of values.

Referring to personal circumstances would be a breach of good manners. Praising my home, still more unsuitable. Nevertheless it is sometimes indispensable, to the extent that such interferences assist in seeing a certain state of things more clearly. This is the case today.

Dear friends, it has been granted to me to write in a language that is spoken only by a few million people. But a language spoken without interruption, with very few differences, throughout more than two thousand five hundred years. This apparently surprising spatial-temporal distance is found in the cultural dimensions of my country. Its spatial area is one of the smallest; but its temporal extension is infinite. If I remind you of this, it is certainly not to derive some kind of pride from it, but to show the difficulties a poet faces when he must make use, to name the things dearest to him, of the same words as did Sappho, for example, or Pindar, while being deprived of the audience they had and which then extended to all of human civilization.

If language were not such a simple means of communication there would not be any problem. But it happens, at times, that it is also an instrument of "magic". In addition, in the course of centuries, language acquires a certain way of being. It becomes a lofty speech. And this way of being entails obligations.

Let us not forget either that in each of these twenty-five centuries and without any interruption, poetry has been written in Greek. It is this collection of given facts which makes the great weight of tradition that this instrument lifts. Modern Greek poetry gives an expressive image of this.

The sphere formed by this poetry shows, one could say, two poles: at one of these poles is Dionysios Solomos, who, before Mallarmé appeared in European literature, managed to formulate, with the greatest rigor and coherency, the concept of pure poetry: to submit sentiment to intelligence, ennoble expression, mobilize all the possibilities of the linguistic instrument by orienting oneself to the miracle. At the other pole is Cavafy, who like T. S. Eliot reaches, by eliminating all form of turgidity, the extreme limit of concision and the most rigorously exact expression.

Between these two poles, and more or less close to one or the other, our other great poets move: Kostis Palamas, Angelos Sikelianos, Nikos Kazantzakis, George Seferis.

Such is, rapidly and schematically drawn, the picture of neo-Hellenic poetic discourse.

We who have followed have had to take over the lofty precept which has been bequeathed to us and adapt it to contemporary sensibility. Beyond the limits of technique, we have had to reach a synthesis, which, on the one hand, assimilated the elements of Greek tradition and, on the other, the social and psychological requirements of our time.

In other words, we had to grasp today's European-Greek in all its truth and turn that truth to account. I do not speak of successes, I speak of intentions, efforts. Orientations have their significance in the investigation of literary history.

But how can creation develop freely in these directions when the conditions of life, in our time, annihilate the creator? And how can a cultural community be created when the diversity of languages raises an unsurpassable obstacle? We know you and you know us through the 20 or 30 per cent that remains of a work after translation. This holds even more true for all those of us who, prolonging the furrow traced by Solomos, expect a miracle from discourse and that a spark flies from between two words with the right sound and in the right position.

No. We remain mute, incommunicable.

We are suffering from the absence of a common language. And the consequences of this absence can be seen — I do not believe I am exaggerating — even in the political and social reality of our common homeland, Europe.

We say — and make the observation each day — that we live in a moral chaos. And this at a moment when — as never before — the allocation of that which concerns our material existence is done in the most systematic manner, in an almost military order, with implacable controls. This contradiction is significant. Of two parts of the body, when one is hypertrophic, the other atrophies. A praise-worthy tendency, encouraging the peoples of Europe to unite, is confronted today with the impossibility of harmonization of the atrophied and hypertrophic parts of our civilization. Our values do not constitute a common language.

For the poet — this may appear paradoxical but it is true — the only common language he still can use is his sensations. The manner in which two bodies are attracted to each other and unite has not changed for millennia. In addition, it has not given rise to any conflict, contrary to the scores of ideologies that have bloodied our societies and have left us with empty hands.

When I speak of sensations, I do not mean those, immediately perceptible, on the first or second level. I mean those which carry us to the extreme edge of ourselves. I also mean the "analogies of sensations" that are formed in our spirits.

For all art speaks through analogy. A line, straight or curved, a sound, sharp or low-pitched, translate a certain optical or acoustic contact. We all write good or bad poems to the extent that we live or reason according to the good or bad meaning of the term. An image of the sea, as we find it in Homer, comes to us intact. Rimbaud will say "a sea mixed with sun". Except he will add: "that is eternity." A young girl holding a myrtle branch in Archilochus survives in a painting by Matisse. And thus the Mediterranean idea of purity is made more tangible to us. In any case, is the image of a virgin in Byzantine iconography so different from that of her secular sisters? Very little is needed for the light of this world to be transformed into supernatural clarity, and inversely. One sensation inherited from the Ancients and another bequeathed by the Middle Ages give birth to a third, one that resembles them both, as a child does its parents. Can poetry survive such a path? Can sensations, at the end of this incessant purification process, reach a state of sanctity? They will return then, as analogies, to graft themselves on the material world and to act on it.

It is not enough to put our dreams into verse. It is too little. It is not enough to politicize our speech. It is too much. The material world is really only an accumulation of materials. It is for us to show ourselves to be good or bad architects, to build Paradise or Hell. This is what poetry never ceases affirming to us — and particularly in these dürftiger times — just this: that in spite of everything our destiny lies in our hands.

I have often tried to speak of solar metaphysics. I will not try today to analyse how art is implicated in such a conception. I will keep to one single and simple fact: the language of the Greeks, like a magic instrument, has — as a reality or a symbol — intimate relations with the Sun. And that Sun does not only inspire a certain attitude of life, and hence the primeval sense to the poem. It penetrates the composition, the structure, and — to use a current terminology — the nucleus from which is composed the cell we call the poem.

It would be a mistake to believe that it is a question of a return to the notion of pure form. The sense of form, as the West has bequeathed it to us, is a constant attainment, represented by three or four models. Three or four moulds, one could say, where it was suitable to pour the most anomalous material at any price. Today that is no longer conceivable. I was one of the first in Greece to break those ties.

What interested me, obscurely at the beginning, then more and more consciously, was the edification of that material according to an architectural model that varied each time. To understand this there is no need to refer to the wisdom of the Ancients who conceived the Parthenons. It is enough to evoke the humble builders of our houses and of our chapels in the Cyclades, finding on each occasion the best solution. Their solutions. Practical and beautiful at the same time, so that in seeing them Le Corbusier could only admire and bow.

Perhaps it is this instinct that woke in me when, for the first time, I had to face a great composition like "Axion Esti." I understood then that without giving the work the proportions and perspective of an edifice, it would never reach the solidity I wished.

I followed the example of Pindar or of the Byzantine Romanos Melodos who, in each of their odes or canticles, invented a new mode for each occasion. I saw that the determined repetition, at intervals, of certain elements of versification effectively gave to my work that multifaceted and symmetrical substance which was my plan.

But then is it not true that the poem, thus surrounded by elements that gravitate around it, is transformed into a little Sun? This perfect correspondence, which I thus find obtained with the intended contents, is, I believe, the poet's most lofty ideal.

To hold the Sun in one's hands without being burned, to transmit it like a torch to those following, is a painful act but, I believe, a blessed one. We have need of it. One day the dogmas that hold men in chains will be dissolved before a consciousness so inundated with light that it will be one with the Sun, and it will arrive on those ideal shores of human dignity and liberty.

Literature 1980

CZESŁAW MIŁOSZ

"who with uncompromising clear-sightedness voices man's exposed condition in a world of severe conflicts"

THE NOBEL PRIZE FOR LITERATURE

Speech by Professor LARS GYLLENSTEN, of the Swedish Academy
Translation from the Swedish text

Your Majesty, Your Royal Highnesses, Ladies and Gentlemen,

Czesław Miłosz was born in Lithuania and grew up in an environment in which primitive folk traditions lived on together with a complex historical heritage. Industrialization had not made itself felt in earnest. People lived in close contact with a still unspoilt nature. This culture and most of its people no longer exist. The Nazi terror and genocide, war and oppression have wreaked devastation.

Miłosz took an early interest in literature and became one of the leading writers in the young generation who wanted to renew poetry and who took an active part in underground freedom movements against the Nazi tyranny. As a socialist he was attached to the new Poland's intellectual élite, becoming in time a trusted cultural person who represented his country abroad. However, the political climate changed during the cold war in a Stalinistic direction. With his uncompromising demand for artistic integrity and human freedom Miłosz could no longer support the régime. In 1951 he left Poland and settled in Paris as a "free writer" — a term not without ironic overtones. In 1960 he moved to USA as a lecturer on Polish literature at Berkeley University. His roots in Poland and his connections with its intellectual life have, however, never been broken.

Disruption and breaking up have marked Miłosz's life from the very beginning. In both an outward and an inward sense he is an exiled writer — a stranger for whom the physical exile is really a reflection of a metaphysical or even religious exile applying to humanity in general. The world that Miłosz depicts in his poetry and prose, works and essays is the world in which man lives after having been driven out of paradise. But the paradise from which he has been banished is not any bleating idyll but a genuine Old Testament Eden for better or worse, with the Serpent as a rival for supremacy. The destructive and treacherous forces are mingled with the good and creative ones — both are equally true and present.

The tensions and contrasts are typical of Miłosz's art and outlook on life. According to him one of the writer's most important tasks is "ouvrir à celui qui le lit une dimension qui rend l'affaire de vivre plus passionnante" — "from galactic silence protect us" and show us "how difficult it is to remain just one person." There is much of the Preacher's or Pascal's fervour in him — a passionate striving to make us intensely aware that we are living scattered abroad and that there *is* no paradise but that evil and havoc are forces to combat. To look reality in the face is not to see everything in darkness and give up in gloom and despair, nor is it to see everything in light and to lapse into escapism and delusion. Still less is it to blur the contours and the focus in favour of convenience or compromise. The tensions, the passion, the contrasts − the diaspora at once freely acknowledged and enforced − are the true meaning of our human condition.

Miłosz is a very intellectual writer, trained in philosophy and literature. His writing is full of voices and references, pastiches and ironies, breaches of style and roles. It is polyphonic in its structure.

But he is also a very sensual writer. One cannot hope to find the rhythmical qualities and the linguistic sensuousness justly reproduced in translation. But the inherent sensuality is there in full measure. His imagery has the character of surprise that only experience can give − that which is experienced in the empirical world, the imagination or memory. The intellectual trait in Miłosz has a direct counterpart in this talent for lucidity and this requited love of the sensuous. In proximity to concrete reality and in human traditions and fellowship he seeks a defence against the destructive forces that hold sway in the world to which we are delivered against our will. Distance and presence characterize him in like degree. The same applies to his relationship to his new country, where he is a writer who must be translated to be understood and who *is* understood and valued, though perhaps in a roundabout way and in incomplete reproductions. He holds that in fact this is something that concerns us all, writers or not.

Strong passions but also strict discipline and unerring perspicacity mark Miłosz's work. An implacable fervour never lets him reconcile himself to man's powerlessness, to the tendency of language towards tricks of illusion and the failures of sympathy, to "remorse that we did not love the poor ashes in Sachsenhausen with absolute love, beyound human power." This fervour of his combines with a mature and sorely tried man's broadmindedness and with a striving for self-control and a stoic or even Epicurean heroism. One comes across outbursts of defiance and rage − almost Nietzschean in their frenzy against the conditions of creation which compel man to be nothing but a man, unable − as the gods can − to change what is mean and cruel. Against this are contrasted moments of calmly clarified repose in what is merely simple and present − miraculously present. His writing is many-voiced and dramatic, insistent and provocative, changing between different moods and levels, from the elegiac to the furious and from the abstract to the extremely concrete.

Czesław Miłosz is a difficult writer, in the best sense of the word – challenging and demanding, captivating not least because of his complications.

Dear Mr. Miłosz! You have sometimes spoken of your language, Polish, as a small language of a rather small people, unknown to most of the world. I have tried to comment upon your life, views and experiences, documented in Polish and nourished on Polish traditions and culture. I have spoken in a still smaller language, still less known to the rest of the world and rather alien from Polish traditions. And I have had a very short time at my disposal to try to describe some of the experiences when reading you. Now I will conclude in English – a language which is neither yours nor mine – and in a still shorter time. Of course I am not able to do justice to you – not at all.

There is a certain irony in the situation — an irony not out of place in this connection. You have often pictured human conditions as basically alienated — we are foreigners in this world and foreigners to one another. But not *only* foreigners. The Nobel Prize to you is also a token and a proof of the fact that borders *may* be crossed, understanding and sympathy fostered, and animating, living contacts or correspondences created. To read your writings and be confronted with their challenges, means to become enriched with important, new experiences — in spite of all alienation.

It is my great pleasure to express the heartfelt congratulations of the Swedish Academy and to ask you to receive this year's Nobel Prize for Literature from the hands of His Majesty the King.

CZESŁAW MIŁOSZ

Czesław Miłosz was born June 30, 1911 in Šeteiniai, Lithuania, as a son of Aleksander Miłosz, a civil engineer, and Weronika, née Kunat. He made his high-school and university studies in Wilno, then belonging to Poland. A co-founder of a literary group "Zagary", he made his literary début in 1930, published in the 1930s two volumes of poetry and worked for the Polish Radio. Most of the war time he spent in Warsaw working there for the underground presses. In the diplomatic service of the People's Poland since 1945, he broke with the government in 1951 and settled in France where he wrote several books in prose. In 1953 he received Prix Littéraire Européen. In 1960, invited by the University of California, he moved to Berkeley where he has been, since 1961, Professor of Slavic Languages and Literatures. Presented with an award for poetry translations from the Polish P.E.N. Club in Warsaw in 1974; a Guggenheim Fellow for poetry 1976; received a honorary degree Doctor of Letters from the University of Michigan, Ann Arbor, in 1977; won the Neustadt International Prize for Literature in 1978; received the "Berkeley Citation" (an equivalent of a honorary Ph.D.) in 1978; nominated by the Academic Senate a "Research Lecturer" of 1979/1980.

NOBEL LECTURE

8 December, 1980
by
CZESŁAW MIŁOSZ
The University of California, Berkeley, USA

I.

My presence here, on this tribune, should be an argument for all those who praise life's God-given, marvelously complex, unpredictability. In my school years I used to read volumes of a series then published in Poland — *The Library of the Nobel Laureates.* I remember the shape of the letters and the color of the paper. I imagined then that the Nobel laureates were writers, namely persons who write thick works in prose, and even when I learned that there were also poets among them, for a long time I could not get rid of that notion. And certainly, when, in 1930, I published my first poems in our university review, *Alma Mater Vilnensis*, I did not aspire to the title of a writer. Also much later, by choosing solitude and giving myself to a strange occupation, that is, to writing poems in Polish while living in France or America, I tried to maintain a certain ideal image of a poet, who, if he wants fame, he wants to be famous only in the village or the town of his birth.

One of the Nobel laureates whom I read in childhood influenced to a large extent, I believe, my notions of poetry. That was Selma Lagerlöf. Her *Wonderful Adventures of Nils*, a book I loved, places the hero in a double role. He is the one who flies above the Earth and looks at it *from above* but at the same time sees it in every detail. This double vision may be a metaphor of the poet's vocation. I found a similar metaphor in a Latin ode of a Seventeenth-Century poet, Maciej Sarbiewski, who was once known all over Europe under the pen-name of Casimire. He taught poetics at my university. In that ode he describes his voyage — on the back of Pegasus — from Vilno to Antwerp, where he is going to visit his poet-friends. Like Nils Holgersson he beholds under him rivers, lakes, forests, that is, a map, both distant and yet concrete. Hence, two attributes of the poet: avidity of the eye and the desire to describe that which he sees. Yet, whoever considers poetry as "to see and to describe" should be aware that he engages in a quarrel with modernity, fascinated as it is with innumerable theories of a specific poetic language.

Every poet depends upon generations who wrote in his native tongue; he inherits styles and forms elaborated by those who lived before him. At the same time, though, he feels that those old means of expression are not adequate to his own experience. When adapting himself, he hears an internal voice that warns him against mask and disguise. But when rebelling, he falls in turn into dependence upon his contemporaries, various movements of the avant-garde. Alas, it is enough for him to publish his first volume of poems, to find himself entrapped. For hardly has the print dried, when that work, which seemed to him the most personal, appears to be enmeshed in the style of another. The only way to counter an obscure remorse is to continue searching and to publish a new book, but then everything repeats itself, so there is no end to that chase. And it may happen that leaving books behind as if they were dry snake skins, in a constant escape forward from what has been done in the past, he receives the Nobel Prize.

What is this enigmatic impulse that does not allow one to settle down in the achieved, the finished? I think it is a quest for reality. I give to this word its naïve and solemn meaning, a meaning having nothing to do with philosophical debates of the last few centuries. It is the Earth as seen by Nils from the back of the gander and by the author of the Latin ode from the back of Pegasus. Undoubtedly, that Earth *is* and her riches cannot be exhausted by any description. To make such an assertion means to reject in advance a question we often hear today: "What is reality?", for it is the same as the question of Pontius Pilate: "What is truth?" If among pairs of opposites which we use every day, the opposition of life and death has such an importance, no less importance should be ascribed to the oppositions of truth and falsehood, of reality and illusion.

II.

Simone Weil, to whose writings I am profoundly indebted, says: "Distance is the soul of beauty". Yet sometimes keeping distance is nearly impossible. I am *A Child of Europe*, as the title of one of the my poems admits, but that is a bitter, sarcastic admission. I am also the author of an auto-biographical book which in the French translation bears the title *Une autre Europe*. Undoubtedly, there exist two Europes and it happens that we, inhabitants of the second one, were destined to descend into "the heart of darkness" of the Twentieth Century. I wouldn't know how to speak about poetry in general. I must speak of poetry in its encounter with peculiar circumstances of time and place. Today, from a perspective, we are able to distinguish outlines of the events which by their death-bearing range surpassed all natural disasters known to us, but poetry, mine and my contemporaries', whether of inherited or avant-garde style, was not prepared to cope with those catastrophes. Like blind men we groped our way and were exposed to all the temptations the mind deluded itself with in our time.

It is not easy to distinguish reality from illusion, especially when one lives in a period of the great upheaval that begun a couple of centuries ago on a small western peninsula of the Euro-Asiatic continent, only to encompass the whole planet during one man's lifetime with the uniform worship of science and technology. And it was particularly difficult to oppose multiple intellectual temptations in those areas of Europe where degenerate ideas of dominion over men, akin to the ideas of dominion over Nature, led to paroxysms of revolution and war at the expense of millions of human beings destroyed physically or spiritually. And yet perhaps our most precious acquisition is not an understanding of those ideas, which we touched in their most tangible shape, but respect and gratitude for certain things which protect people from internal disintegration and from yielding to tyranny. Precisely for that reason some ways of life, some institutions became a target for the fury of evil forces, above all, the bonds between people that exist organically, as if by themselves, sustained by family, religion, neighborhood, common heritage. In other words, all that disorderly, illogical humanity, so often branded as ridiculous because of its parochial attachments and loyalties. In many countries traditional bonds of *civitas* have been subject to a gradual erosion and their inhabitants become disinherited without realizing it. It is not the same, however, in those areas where suddenly, in a situation of utter peril, a protective, life-giving value of such bonds reveals itself. That is the case of my native land. And I feel this is a proper place to mention gifts received by myself and by my friends in our part of Europe and to pronounce words of blessing.

It is good to be born in a small country where Nature was on a human scale, where various languages and religions cohabited for centuries. I have in mind Lithuania, a country of myths and of poetry. My family already in the Sixteenth Century spoke Polish, just as many families in Finland spoke Swedish and in Ireland — English; so I am a Polish, not a Lithuanian, poet. But the landscapes and perhaps the spirits of Lithuania have never abandoned me. It is good in childhood to hear words of Latin liturgy, to translate Ovid in high school, to receive a good training in Roman Catholic dogmatics and apologetics. It is a blessing if one receives from fate school and university studies in such a city as Vilno. A bizarre city of baroque architecture transplanted to northern forests and of history fixed in every stone, a city of forty Roman Catholic churches and of numerous synagogues. In those days the Jews called it a Jerusalem of the North. Only when teaching in America did I fully realize how much I had absorbed from the thick walls of our ancient university, from formulas of Roman law learned by heart, from history and literature of old Poland, both of which surprise young Americans by their specific features: an indulgent anarchy, a humor disarming fierce quarrels, a sense of organic community, a mistrust of any centralized authority.

A poet who grew up in such a world should have been a seeker for reality through contemplation. A patriarchal order should have been dear to him, a sound of bells, an isolation from pressures and the persistent demands of his fellow men, silence of a cloister cell. If books were to linger on a table, then they should be those which deal with the most incomprehensible quality of God-created things, namely being, the *esse*. But suddenly all this is negated by demoniac doings of History which acquires the traits of a blood-thirsty Deity. The Earth which the poet viewed in his flight calls with a cry, indeed, out of the abyss and doesn't allow itself to be viewed *from above*. An insoluble contradiction appears, a terribly real one, giving no peace of mind either day or night, whatever we call it, it is the contradiction between being and action, or, on another level, a contradiction between art and solidarity with one's fellow men. Reality calls for a name, for words, but it is unbearable and if it is touched, if it draws very close, the poet's mouth cannot even utter a complaint of Job: all art proves to be nothing compared with action. Yet, to embrace reality in such a manner that it is preserved in all its old tangle of good and evil, of despair and hope, is possible only thanks to a distance, only by soaring *above* it — but this in turn seems then a moral treason.

Such was the contradiction at the very core of conflicts engendered by the Twentieth Century and discovered by poets of an Earth polluted by the crime of genocide. What are the thoughts of one of them, who wrote a certain number of poems which remain as a memorial, as a testimony? He thinks that they were born out of a painful contradiction and that he would prefer to have been able to resolve it while leaving them unwritten.

III.

A patron saint of all poets in exile, who visit their towns and provinces only in remembrance, is always Dante. But how has the number of Florences increased! The exile of a poet is today a simple function of a relatively recent discovery: that whoever wields power is also able to control language and not only with the prohibitions of censorship, but also by changing the meaning of words. A peculiar phenomenon makes its appearance: the language of a captive community acquires certain durable habits; whole zones of reality cease to exist simply because they have no name. There is, it seems, a hidden link between theories of literature as *Écriture*, of speech feeding on itself, and the growth of the totalitarian state. In any case, there is no reason why the state should not tolerate an activity that consists of creating "experimental" poems and prose, if these are conceived as auto-nomous systems of reference, enclosed within their own boundaries. Only if we assume that a poet constantly strives to liberate himself from borrowed styles in search for reality, is he dangerous. In a room where people unanimously maintain a conspiracy of silence, one word of truth sounds like a pistol shot. And, alas, a temptation to pronounce it, similar to an acute itching, becomes an obsession which doesn't allow one to think of anything else. That is why a poet chooses internal or external exile. It is not certain, however, that he is motivated exclusively by his concern with actuality. He may also desire to free himself from it and elsewhere, in other countries, on other shores, to recover, at least for short moments, his true vocation — which is to contemplate Being.

That hope is illusory, for those who come from the "other Europe", wherever they find themselves, notice to what extent their experiences isolate them from their new milieu — and this may become the source of a new obsession. Our planet that gets smaller every year, with its fantastic proliferation of mass media, is witnessing a process that escapes definition, characterized by a refusal to remember. Certainly, the illiterates of past centuries, then an enormous majority of mankind, knew little of the history of their respective countries and of their civilization. In the minds of modern illiterates, however, who know how to read and write and even teach in schools and at universities, history is present but blurred, in a state of strange confusion; Molière becomes a contemporary of Napoleon, Voltaire, a contemporary of Lenin. Also, events of the last decades, of such primary importance that knowledge or ignorance of them will be decisive for the future of mankind, move away, grow pale, lose all consistency as if Frederic Nietzsche's prediction of European nihilism found a literal fulfillment. "The eye of a nihilist" — he wrote in 1887 — "is unfaithful to his memories: it allows them to drop, to lose their leaves; ... And what he does not do for himself, he also does not do for the whole past of mankind: he lets it drop". We are surrounded today by fictions about the past, contrary to common sense and to an elementary perception of good and evil. As "The Los Angeles Times" recently stated, the number of books in various languages which deny that the Holocaust ever took place, that it was invented by Jewish propaganda, has exceeded one hundred. If such an insanity is possible, is a complete loss of memory as a permanent state of mind improbable? And would it not present a danger more grave than genetic engineering or poisoning of the natural environment?

For the poet of the "other Europe" the events embraced by the name of the Holocaust are a reality, so close in time that he cannot hope to liberate himself from their remembrance unless, perhaps, by translating the Psalms of David. He feels anxiety, though, when the meaning of the word Holocaust undergoes gradual modifications, so that the word begins to belong to the history of the Jews exclusively, as if among the victims there were not also millions of Poles, Russians, Ukrainians and prisoners of other nationalities. He feels anxiety, for he senses in this a foreboding of a not distant future when history will be reduced to what appears on television, while the truth, as it is too complicated, will be buried in the archives, if not totally annihilated. Other facts as well, facts for him quite close but distant for the West, add in his mind to the credibility of H. G. Wells' vision in *The Time Machine*: the Earth inhabited by a tribe of children of the day, carefree, deprived of memory and, by the same token, of history, without defense when confronted with dwellers of subterranean caves, cannibalistic children of the night.

Carried forward, as we are, by the movement of technological change, we realize that the unification of our planet is in the making and we attach importance to the notion of international community. The days when the League of Nations and the United Nations were founded deserve to be remembered. Unfortunately, those dates lose their significance in comparison with another date which should be invoked every year as a day of mourning, while it is hardly known to younger generations. It is the date of 23 August, 1939. Two dictators then concluded an agreement provided with a secret clause by the virtue of which they divided between themselves neighboring countries possessing their own capitals, governments and parliaments. That pact not only unleashed a terrible war; it re-established a colonial principle, according to which nations are not more than cattle, bought, sold, completely dependent upon the will of their instant masters. Their borders, their right to self-determination, their passports ceased to exist. And it should be a source of wonder that today people speak in a whisper, with a finger to their lips, about how that principle was applied by the dictators forty years ago.

Crimes against human rights, never confessed and never publicly denounced, are a poison which destroys the possibility of a friendship between nations. Anthologies of Polish poetry publish poems of my late friends — Wladyslaw Sebyla and Lech Piwowar, and give the date of their deaths: 1940. It is absurd not to be able to write how they perished, though everybody in Poland knows the truth: they shared the fate of several thousand Polish officers disarmed and interned by the then accomplices of Hitler, and they repose in a mass grave. And should not the young generations of the West, if they study history at all, hear about the 200,000 people killed in 1944 in Warsaw, a city sentenced to annihilation by those two accomplices?

The two genocidal dictators are no more and yet, who knows whether they did not gain a victory more durable than those of their armies. In spite of the Atlantic Charter, the principle that nations are objects of trade, if not chips in games of cards or dice, has been confirmed by the division of Europe into two zones. The absence of the three Baltic states from the United Nations is a permanent reminder of the two dictators' legacy. Before the war those states belonged to the League of Nations but they disappeared from the map of Europe as a result of the secret clause in the agreement of 1939.

I hope you forgive my laying bare a memory like a wound. This subject is not unconnected with my meditation on the word "reality", so often misused but always deserving esteem. Complaints of peoples, pacts more treacherous than those we read about in Thucydides, the shape of a maple leaf, sunrises and sunsets over the ocean, the whole fabric of causes and effects, whether we call it Nature or History, points towards, I believe, another hidden reality, impenetrable, though exerting a powerful attraction that is the central driving force of all art and science. There are moments when it seems to me that I decipher the meaning of afflictions which befell the nations of the "other Europe" and that meaning is to make them the bearers of memory — at the time when Europe, without an adjective, and America possess it less and less with every generation.

It is possible that there is no other memory than the memory of wounds. At least we are so taught by the Bible, a book of the tribulations of Israel. That book for a long time enabled European nations to preserve a sense of continuity — a word not to be mistaken for the fashionable term, historicity.

During the thirty years I have spent abroad I have felt I was more privileged than my Western colleagues, whether writers or teachers of literature, for events both recent and long past took in my mind a sharply delineated, precise form. Western audiences confronted with poems or novels written in Poland, Czechoslovakia or Hungary, or with films produced there, possibly intuit a similarly sharpened consciousness, in a constant struggle against limitations imposed by censorship. Memory thus is our force, it protects us against a speech entwining upon itself like the ivy when it does not find a support on a tree or a wall.

A few minutes ago I expressed my longing for the end of a contradiction which opposes the poet's need of distance to his feeling of solidarity with his fellow men. And yet, if we take a flight *above* the Earth as a metaphor of the poet's vocation, it is not difficult to notice that a kind of contradiction is implied, even in those epochs when the poet is relatively free from the snares of History. For how to be *above* and simultaneously to see the Earth in every detail? And yet, in a precarious balance of opposites, a certain equilibrium can be achieved thanks to a distance introduced by the flow of time. "To see" means not only to have before one's eyes. It may mean also to preserve in memory. "To see and to describe" may also mean to reconstruct in imagination. A distance achieved, thanks to the mystery of time, must not change events, landscapes, human figures into a tangle of shadows growing paler and paler. On the contrary, it can show them in full light, so that every event, every date becomes expressive and persists as an eternal reminder of human depravity and human greatness. Those who are alive receive a mandate from those who are silent forever. They can fulfill their duties only by trying to reconstruct precisely things as they were, and by wresting the past from fictions and legends.

Thus both — the Earth seen from above in an eternal now and the Earth that endures in a recovered time — may serve as material for poetry.

IV.

I would not like to create the impression that my mind is turned toward the past, for that would not be true. Like all my contemporaries I have felt the pull of despair, of impending doom, and reproached myself for succumbing to a nihilistic temptation. Yet on a deeper level, I believe, my poetry remained sane and, in a dark age, expressed a longing for the Kingdom of Peace and Justice. The name of a man who taught me not to despair should be invoked here. We receive gifts not only from our native land, its lakes and rivers, its traditions, but also from people, especially if we meet a powerful personality in our early youth. It was my good fortune to be treated nearly as a son by my relative Oscar Milosz, a Parisian recluse and a visionary. Why he was a French poet, could be elucidated by the intricate story of a family as well as of a country once called the Grand Duchy of Lithuania. Be that as it may, it was possible to read recently in the Parisian press words of regret that the highest international distinction had not been awarded half a century earlier to a poet bearing the same family name as my own.

I learned much from him. He gave me a deeper insight into the religion of the Old and New Testament and inculcated a need for a strict, ascetic hierarchy in all matters of mind, including everything that pertains to art, where as a major sin he considered putting the second-rate on the same level with the first-rate. Primarily, though, I listened to him as a prophet who loved people, as he says, "with old love worn out by pity, loneliness and anger" and for that reason tried to address a warning to a crazy world rushing towards a catastrophe. That a catastrophe was imminent, I heard from him, but also I heard from him that the great conflagration he predicted would be merely a part of a larger drama to be played to the end.

He saw deeper causes in an erroneous direction taken by science in the Eighteenth Century, a direction which provoked landslide effects. Not unlike William Blake before him, he announced a New Age, a second renaissance of imagination now polluted by a certain type of scientific knowledge, but, as he believed, not by all scientific knowledge, least of all by science that would be discovered by men of the future. And it does not matter to what extent I took his predictions literally: a general orientation was enough.

Oscar Milosz, like William Blake, drew inspirations from the writings of Emanuel Swedenborg, a scientist who, earlier than anyone else, foresaw the defeat of man, hidden in the Newtonian model of the Universe. When, thanks to my relative, I became an attentive reader of Swedenborg, interpreting him not, it is true, as was common in the Romantic era, I did not imagine I would visit his country for the first time on such an occasion as the present one.

Our century draws to its close, and largely thanks to those influences I would not dare to curse it, for it has also been a century of faith and hope. A profound transformation, of which we are hardly aware, because we are a part of it, has been taking place, coming to the surface from time to time in phenomena that provoke general astonishment. That transformation has to do, and I use here words of Oscar Milosz, with "the deepest secret of toiling masses, more than ever alive, vibrant and tormented". Their secret, an unavowed need of true values, finds no language to express itself and here not only the mass media but also intellectuals bear a heavy responsibility. But transformation has been going on, defying short term predictions, and it is probable that in spite of all horrors and perils, our time will be judged as a necessary phase of travail before mankind ascends to a new awareness. Then a new hierarchy of merits will emerge, and I am convinced that Simone Weil and Oscar Milosz, writers in whose school I obediently studied, will receive their due. I feel we should publicly confess our attachment to certain names because in that way we define our position more forcefully than by pronouncing the names of those to whom we would like to address a violent "no". My hope is that in this lecture, in spite of my meandering thought, which is a professional bad habit of poets, my "yes" and "no" are clearly stated, at least as to the choice of succession. For we all who are here, both the speaker and you who listen, are no more than links between the past and the future.